W9-CGR-653

THE FORTY-FIRST ANNUAL **TYPE DIRECTORS CLUB** EXHIBITION

T6

TYPOGRAPHY

CIRCA

TYPOG

1 6 9

THE
ANNUAL
OF
THE

TYPE DIREC

R A P H Y

95

TORS CLUB

WATSON·GUPTILL PUBLICATIONS NEW YORK

EXHIBITION 1ST

Copyright ©1995 by the Type Directors Club

First published in 1995 by
Watson-Guptill Publications,
a division of BPI Communications, Inc.,
1515 Broadway, New York, NY 10036.

The Library of Congress has cataloged
this serial title as follows:
Typography (Type Directors Club [U.S.])
Typography: the annual of the
Type Directors Club.—|—
New York: Watson-Guptill
Publications, 1980—
v.ill.;29 cm

Annual.
ISSN 0275—6870 = Typography (New York, N.Y.)
1. Printing, Practical—Periodicals.
2. Graphic arts—periodicals.
1. Type Directors Club (U.S.).
Z243.A2T9a 686.2'24 81—640363
AACR 2 MARC-S
Library of Congress [8605]

Distributed in the United Kingdom by
Phaidon Press, Ltd., 140 Kensington Church
Street, London W8 4BN, England.

Distributed in Europe (except the United
Kingdom), South and Central America,
the Caribbean, the Far East, the Southeast,
and Central Asia by Rotovision S.A., Route
Suisse 9, CH-1295 Mies, Switzerland.

All rights reserved. No part of this
publication may be reproduced or used in
any form or by any means—graphic,
electronic, or mechanical, including photo-
copying, recording, taping, or information
storage and retrieval systems—without
written permission of the publisher.

Manufactured in Singapore

First printing, 1995

1 2 3 4 5 6 7 8 9 /02 01 00 99 98 97 96 95

Acknowledgments

The Type Directors Club gratefully acknowledges
the following for their enthusiastic support
and contributions to the success of TDC41:

Design: Drenttel Doyle Partners
Exhibition facilities: The Arthur A. Houghton Jr.
    Gallery at The Cooper Union
Judging facilities: School of Visual Arts
Paper: S.D. Warren
Printer (Call for Entries): Quality House of Graphics
Computer hardware: Nancy Carr, Market
    Development Executive, Apple Computer
Chairperson and Executive Director Photography:
    Keith Trumbo
Judges Photography (not included): Dick Frank

Senior Editor: Marian Appellof
Associate Editor: Micaela Porta
Design Coordinator: Jay Anning
Production Manager: Ellen Greene

CONTENTS

6

6 To say that I was delighted and flattered when I was invited to chair the 41st Type Directors Club competition would be an understatement. When it came to the reality, however, I was somewhat in shock. This turned out to be a pretty strange year in many respects and I wondered more than once whether or not I had been crazy to take on this responsibility.

Like the politicians say, it was a year of change. And the greatest changes this year resulted from the developments in multimedia technology. Members of the design profession were intrigued by the results of new interactive software programs which combined photography, illustration, audio, video, and, of course, typography.

It was a year in which being cool meant you talked a lot about diversity and boundaries and bragged about being connected to the World Wide Web, even though you weren't quite sure what (and where) it was. It was also a time when everyone was experimenting with what seemed like a thousand new typefaces, some weird, some wonderful, and quite a few that defied description.

Many designers were creating their own typefaces and modifying others, while a lot of other people who didn't know a pica from a Leica were collecting fonts like they were baseball cards. All in all, it started to feel like the whole world was in a type frenzy, and that was both good and bad news.

I found myself in a rather tenuous position. In an aesthetic and philosophical environment where the operational rule is that there are no rules, who determines which work is the very best? And how does a typography competition reward excellence when the very criteria for excellence are in the process of being redefined?

At some point it became obvious that what was needed to make this competition really work was a "dream team," a group of prominent designers whose judgment would be respected by everyone. Somehow, we managed to pull it off.

Stephen Doyle miraculously consented to design the Call for Entries and the Annual as well as to serve as a judge. Gail Anderson, Michael Bierut, Neville Brody, Alex Isley, Gary Koepke, and Jennifer Morla graciously agreed to judge the competition as well. We were on our way.

The rest, as they say, is history. The judging was very professional. Every one of the 2,894 international entries was given careful consideration by each judge.

At the end, when the judges met as a group to review the selected pieces, everyone expressed satisfaction with both the individual choices and the overall look of the show. Their efforts were a considerable accomplishment.

Many people contributed to the success of TDC41. I would like to thank the wonderful judges, the board of the Type Directors Club, the many members who were kind enough to put in long hours, and my students from the Parsons School of Design who worked so speedily that we broke the record and completed judging ahead of schedule. I especially want to express my gratitude to my associate and dear friend, Carol Wahler, who held my hand every step of the way.

What follows are the 239 entries which comprise the largest Type Directors Club show in TDC's history. After you have had an opportunity to see them all, I would appreciate your taking a few minutes to let me know what you think. My e-mail address is: MKstudiol@aol.com. You can also reach me by snail mail at the Type Directors Club, 60 East 42nd Street, Suite 721, New York, NY 10165. I look forward to hearing from you.

Mara Kurtz is a graphic designer, illustrator, and photographer who runs her own design company, Mara Kurtz Studio. Her photographs and hand-tinted photo collages appear regularly in Metropolis and The New York Times Magazine. She has received awards from the AIGA Graphic Design USA Annual, Creativity, Communication Arts, Graphis, Print Regional Design Annual, the Society of Illustrators, and the Society of Publication Designers.

A member of the Type Directors Club board for two years, Kurtz is currently serving her second term as the club's Vice President. She also heads the Scholarship Committee, is Co-Chair of the Program Committee, and contributes articles and book reviews to Letterspace, the TDC newsletter. She was awarded the 1994 Fellowship Award for the Type Directors Club given by the New York Printing House Craftsmen.

Kurtz is a faculty member of the Parsons School of Design where she teaches advanced graphic design, collage, photography, and typography. She is a member of the Graphic Design Educators Association and Photographers of the Motion Picture and Television Industries. A graduate of the New York University Film School and the Parsons School of Design, Kurtz is now a candidate for a Master's Degree in Media Studies at The New School.

Since 1987, Gail Anderson has served as Deputy Art Director of *Rolling Stone* magazine. Previously she was a graphic designer at *The Boston Globe Magazine* and at Vintage Books. Her work has received numerous design competition and publication awards from the AIGA, Art Directors Club, *Communication Arts*, Society of Publication Designers, and the Type Directors Club, and is represented in the permanent collection of the Cooper-Hewitt National Design Museum. She is coauthor with Stephen Heller of *Graphic Wit: The Art of Humor in Design*. Her other books are *The Savage Mirror: The Art of Contemporary Caricature*, and *American Typeplay*, a survey of cotemporary typography. She teaches graphic design at the School of Visual Arts in New York City.

Stephen Doyle is a designer who is known for taking risks, (sometimes in yellow.) Since co-founding Drenttel Doyle Partners with William Drenttel and Tom Kluepfel in 1985, they have received international acclaim for their work for such clients as the Museum of Modern Art, Champion International Corp., the Edison Project, Knopf, Cooper-Hewitt National Design Museum, HarperCollins and others. ID magazine reports that the partners "reject fashionable styles in favor of solid functional approaches rooted in concept, not adornment…all without losing their sense of humor." Doyle is a frequent (and sometimes outspoken) lecturer and has taught design practice at his alma mater, Cooper Union, as well as the graduate program at Yale.

Award-winning designer Michael Bierut has been a partner in the New York office of Pentagram since 1990. His clients include American Ballet Theatre, Disney Development, Godiva Chocolatier, Mohawk Paper Mills, *NewYork* magazine, Nickelodeon, and the Minnesota Children's Museum. Before joining Pentagram he was vice president of graphic design at Vignelli Associates. His work is represented in the permanent collections of museums in New York, Washington D.C, and Montreal. He is a director of the American Center for Design, a member of the *Alliance Graphique Internationale*, and Contributing Editor to the magazine *ID*.

Known for his sense of humor, Alex Isley established his design company in 1988. A graduate of Cooper Union, Isley was formerly senior designer at M&Co. and served as the first full-time art director of *Spy*, which earned him Gold and Silver Medals from the Society of Publication Designers. His firm has created award-winning work for a diverse range of clients: the American Museum of the Moving Image, Giorgio Armani, *Forbes Inc.*, International Typeface Corporation, Mesa Grill, MTV Networks, Nickelodeon, Pepsi, The Rock and Roll Hall of Fame, Time Warner and Little, Brown Publishers. His work has appeared in major design publications and shows and is represented in the permanent collection of the Cooper-Hewitt National Design Museum.

Gary Koepke has designed and directed consumer and corporate magazines, including *Global* for Bull H.N. Information Systems, *26*, a typography magazine for Agfa Corporation, and *Creem* magazine. He created *World Tour* magazine for Dun & Bradstreet Software, designed an issue of Benetton's *Colors* magazine, and helped launch *Vibe* magazine. Currently designing a book of photography and words by David Byrne, Koepke is also acting Creative Director for J. Crew. His work has won him gold and silver medals at the Society of Publication Designers and Art Directors Club of New York, where he won Best of Show in 1993. Adweek named him a creative all-star, and ID magazine a "Top 40 Design Innovator." Koepke's work has been featured in Graphis, Print, Creative Review (England), BáT (France), SH--i-n-c (Japan), Baseline, and ID.

British designer Neville Brody is one of the most influential figures in typography and design today. As art director for the British magazines *Arena*, *The Face*, *City Limits*, and *Tatler*, the Italian publications *Lei* and *Per Lui*, and the French *Actuel*, he was a pioneer in experimental digital type design. He is currently creating an identity program for a German pay-TV channel and designing postage stamps for the Netherlands PTT. Other clients are the Body Shop, Budweiser, CBS, Mont Blanc, the Museum of Modern Art, Nike, and Swatch. A co-founder of FontShop, he develops and publishes many of his own fonts and edits *FUSE*, an experimental digital type magazine. The sequel to the best-selling *The Graphic Language of Neville Brody* was published in 1994

Jennifer Morla is President and Creative Director of Morla Design. She has been honored internationally for her ability to pair wit and elegance on everything from annual reports to music videos. In addition to her over 500 awards for excellence in graphic design, she was declared one of the fifteen masters of design by How magazine. Her work is part of the permanent collection of the San Francisco Museum of Modern Art and the Library of Congress, and has also been displayed at the Grand Palais in Paris and The Brandenburg Art Gallery in Berlin. Most recently, her work was featured in a solo exhibition in Osaka, Japan. In addition to teaching Senior Graphic Design at California College of Arts and Crafts, she paints, sculpts, and creates site-specific installations.

THE JUDGES' CHOICE

I've always loved the posters that Paul Davis produced for the Public Theater, and so by habit I automatically look over at the theater when I cross Astor Place. A few months ago I stopped in my tracks to admire a wonderful banner hanging from the theater. "I wish I'd done that," I thought, in one of those this-is-why-I-love-graphic-design moments. That great wood type, the scale, the wit, the unselfconscious beauty and boldness of it—I just loved it. The type was truly alive.

Over time I discovered what turned out to be a series of new designs for the Public Theater. The work reflected street typography —the letterforms were a bit rough, their baselines a little off. The posters were energetic, streetwise, and accessible; power-ful and yet quick hits that made me think that something new must be going on at the Public Theater.

Then the posters resurfaced at the TDC judging. I wish I could have taken them home, but then I guess that would have made it tough for them to have gotten into the show. I would never have thought I could love any Public Theater posters as much as the Paul Davis paintings, but this new identity program by Pentagram really makes me covet my neighbor's goods.

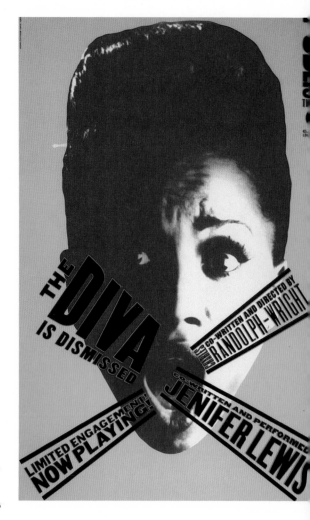

Best known for producing the New York Shakespeare Festival every summer in Central Park, the Public Theater is also one of New York City's leading venues for new theatrical productions.

The theater had long flourished under the directorship of the legendary Joseph Papp; following Papp's death, the traditionally dynamic organiza-tion faltered and lost its edge.

George C. Wolfe's appointment as producer brought new energy to The Public. In Wolfe's vision, The Public Theater would live up to its name by enlarging the scope and diversity of its audience and promoting itself as streetwise, timely, and accessible.

When Papp was producer at The Public, Paul Davis produced a memorable series of illustrated posters which set the standard for theater promotion for nearly a decade. In keeping with the expanded vision of the new producer, a new identity and pro-motional graphics program have been developed to reflect street typography; active, unconventional, and graffiti-like. The posters for the 1994-5 season are based on juxtapositions of photography and type.

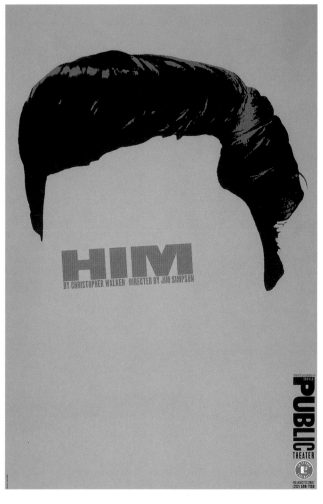

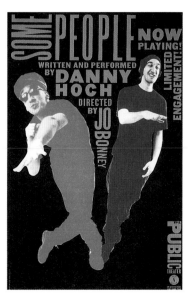

DESIGNER
PAULA SCHER,
RON LOUIE,
AND LISA MAZUR
NEW YORK NEW YORK

TYPOGRAPHIC SOURCE
IN-HOUSE

STUDIO
PENTAGRAM
DESIGN

CLIENT
THE PUBLIC
THEATER

PRINCIPAL TYPES
MORGAN
GOTHIC,
PAULAWOOD,
SERIWOOD,
E TEN,
E SEVENTEEN,
E TWENTY-FIVE,
WOOD BLOCK
CONDENSED,
AND ALTERNATE
GOTHIC NO. 2

DIMENSIONS
30 x 46 IN.

" A fake ain't a fake without a little
SHAKE AND BAKE.*"*
Pee Wee Kirkland

NYC

MICHAEL BIERUT

Many of the entries in this year's competition fell in one of
two directions. The first was a return to classicism: elegant
typography, precise compositions, coolness, white space,
restraint. The other direction was an embrace of rawness:
in-your-face typefaces, nasty headlines, willful dirtiness.

What makes Nike's "NYC" campaign interesting
to me is that it combines both directions. Great, raw black
and white photographs used with the precision of a
Brodovitch. Hilariously vicious putdowns rendered in
exquisite Trajan capitals. Contrast is what New York is all
about, and with this work Wieden & Kennedy nail New
York perfectly.

While this campaign was running, I would pick
my subway car based on how many Nike ads I could see
inside. I think once I even missed my stop.

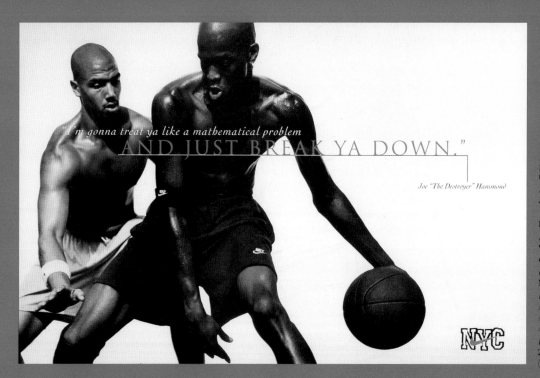

"I'm gonna treat ya like a mathematical problem

AND JUST BREAK YA DOWN."

Joe "The Destroyer" Hammond

DESIGNER
IMIN PAO
PORTLAND OREGON

ART DIRECTOR
JOHN JAY

TYPOGRAPHIC SOURCE
IN-HOUSE

AGENCY
WIEDEN
& KENNEDY

CLIENT
NIKE

PRINCIPAL TYPES
ADOBE TRAJAN
AND
ADOBE COCHIN

DIMENSIONS
25 x 38 IN.
(63.5 x 96.5 CM)

Nowhere does basketball reach such mythical status as in New York City. Here, the sport transforms into a religion, where a single act of superb skill can live for decades beyond the actual moment. Reputations developed on its fabled playgrounds become neighborhood folklore, and through word of mouth, real legends are made.

The Nike "NYC" campaign is a celebration of that special spirit, that love for the sport that transcends today's definition of success. It's a celebration of a unique style of play as well. A style that has power as well as elegance. Like the city itself, it expresses a knack for one-upmanship, a unique verbal skill of storytelling, and a dramatic sense of contrasts.

The "Trash Talk" campaign was just a part of Nike's "NYC" integrated effort. The quotes featured witty examples of on-court "intimidation" from past and present street legends. Players were cast from the playgrounds and as a sign of respect and recognition of their uniqueness, the "NYC" campaign only appears in New York City.

" I'm gonna fake left, go right, bump ya, and then

DUNK ON YOUR ASS."

Earl "Goat" Manigault

NEVILLE BRODY

This project stood out from all of the other entries in this year's TDC competition. It takes the risk and succeeds in its dangerous ambition of covering a wide range of typographic formats and approaches, combining different photographic styles and subjects with different paper stocks and layouts. The basic design of the actual day-to-day diary pages is extremely elegant, recalling a design language associated with the documents produced by the early explorers and map makers. The care taken with each and every detail is clearly evident, and sense of space makes the diary a pleasure to use. Each of the four break sections are a discovery in themselves, exploring different themes in strikingly different ways, imparting a sense of time travel, bringing you to the modern day and beyond. The sections act as a kind of social overview, connecting various obsessions and beliefs in an emotionally simple manner, abstracted to allow the reader to complete the picture for him or herself. This diary is a journey, a process of discovery which reveals a different meaning at each reading. The beautiful images are complemented with a dynamic range of typographic languages which extend to the cover of this square-formatted black-encased volume. On it you find an understated cover title in the form of a small label applied to an embossed typographic container. Excellent typographic treatment. I am going to hold on to my review copy.

DESIGNER
STEVEN TOLLESON
AND JENNIFER
STERLING
SAN FRANCISCO CALIFORNIA

TYPOGRAPHIC SOURCE
IN-HOUSE

STUDIO
TOLLESON DESIGN

CLIENT
FOX RIVER PAPER
COMPANY

PRINCIPAL TYPE
GARAMOND

DIMENSIONS
9¼ x 8½ IN.
(23.5 x 21.6 CM)

The purpose of the project was to create and produce a piece that would demonstrate the production and manufacturing of Confetti as well as attract international design diversity. In addition the piece needed to function in daily life.

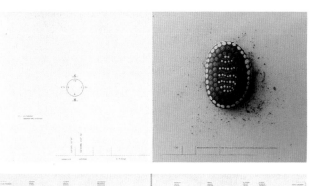

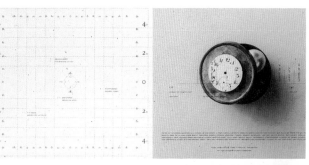

We created a hard-bound desk calendar with a time capsule living within. Conceptually, the idea of a time capsule calendar is based on objects that inspire us and encapsulate the time and place in which we live. For a global feel we then asked three culturally diverse firms to design three pages based on the following subjects: Religion and Philosophy, Daily Life, Music and Literature, and ours, Science and Technology. The calendar was then broken into quarters with the sections commissioned leading each quarter. The metal tin photographed on the cover and intro page holds the three-dimensional item that represents the theme of each culture, while the typographic treatment indicates the geographic location of each culture.

[Stadt Bild

STEPHEN DOYLE

Stadt Bild translates dully to "City Picture," and this oversize book composes a thoughtful portrait of the Frankfurt art scene. Just as the title boldly juxtaposes two simple words, the catalog is a juxtaposition of two books: the first, an elegantly laid out catalog of artworks; the second, a scrappy collage of marked-up old newspaper clippings, letters, photos, and announcements. The saddle-stitched catalog is printed on white, the spiral-bound collage is printed on black. These volumes, bound together, beautifully put its artwork into context. Some of the clippings are about the politics of urban life and some are reviews of artwork. The odd binding has the effect of weaving together these two books, which is an apt metaphor for the artwork being documented. Just as a letter has two lives, one at the writing and one at the reading, this catalog proves that artwork has a life of its own after it is made, beyond the realm of its maker.

Stadt Bild originally was meant to be a catalog documenting an exhibition in Frankfurt. The object of both book and exhibition was to demonstrate the relationship between the city of Frankfurt and art during the last five decades.

The book consists of two parts, one reflecting on some typical artists and showing their work, one demonstrating the reactions of the press and commemorating main events in cultural politics in Frankfurt. The idea was to be able to look at both parts at the same time. This was achieved by the unusual binding.

Old articles from newspapers had been saved (before the decade of microfiches and scanners) in an old-fashioned way: glued on black paper, sometimes with photos and other items. To give this special impression of an old archive, Heine Lenz Zizka chose this form of presentation. The large format derives from that idea — the reader should look at the old articles in their original size.

Some new elements, like the title-logo, well-chosen photographs, and an interesting introduction give the whole book a fresh look.

The design of the entire thing is completely subservient to this powerful pairing. Both volumes ooze restraint to a degree that must be applauded. The designers have surrendered themselves unswervingly to this one simple idea, and have made a powerful and memorable book that lives up to its title. And besides, how can you not love that cover photo?

DESIGNERS
**KLAUS-ACHIM
HEINE, MICHAEL
LENZ, AND
PETER ZIZKA**
FRANKFURT GERMANY

TYPOGRAPHIC SOURCE
**IN-HOUSE AND
UNIVERSITÄTS-
DRUCKEREI
UND VERLAG H.
SCHMIDT MAINZ**

STUDIO
**HEINE, LENZ,
ZIZKA**

CLIENT
**AMT FÜR
WISSENSCHAFT
UND KUNST DER
STADT UND
VERLAG HERMANN
SCHMIDT VERLAG**

PRINCIPAL TYPES
**JOANNA AND
FRANKLIN
GOTHIC**

DIMENSIONS
**12²/₅ x 16¹/₂ IN.
(31.5 x 42 CM)**

thoughtful, communicative, appropriate, and makes me really jealous.

When describing something as thoughtful, communicative, and appropriate, particularly when it's a brochure for a State Toll Highway Authority, a pretty deadly mental image pirouettes into place. But this isn't stiff at all. The designers employed the deceptively simple motif of road signs to serve as a unifying element to great effect. The result is a design that is smart, elegant, and seemingly effortless – a hard thing to pull off (particularly, I would imagine, with a government agency as the client).

I see in this design a great amount of self-confidence on the part of the designers, which makes by extension for a design that reflects well on the client. What this also represents to me is a great deal of behind-the-scenes confidence in the ability of the designers on the part of the clients.

It is important to know that this selection was made as a Judge's favorite without benefit of my knowing any background information concerning budget, or lack of one. Knowing that this piece was created and produced on the cheap makes the achievement even more impressive, and proves once again that a big idea will beat a small budget every time.

MILE
40

In the design of the 1993 Illinois State Toll Highway Authority annual report, the goal was to commemorate the authority's 40th year and review 1993 in an appropriate but striking way—and within an extremely limited budget.

The report reviews the accomplishments of the year in three areas—people, planning, and technology—while contrasting the tollway of today with the tollway of 40 years ago. Significant ink is also devoted to communicating the Authority's vision for the future.

We used a sign motif as our visual theme—using the green color and graphics familiar to everyone who travels the tollway. People shots were scanned and provided on disk by the photographer and silhouetted in-house at VSA to conserve printing dollars. The report was designed, written, and printed for approximately half of what a 32-page report typically costs.

PLANNING

FROM THE DAY IT OPENED, THE TOLLWAY BEGAN
FULFILLING GROWING DEMAND FOR CONVENIENT
HIGHWAY TRANSPORTATION LINKING THE
COMMUNITIES OF NORTHEAST ILLINOIS.
IN 1993, THE AUTHORITY
CONTINUED TO PLAN FOR THE FUTURE.
WE RECEIVED APPROVAL FROM THE STATE
TO PURSUE FOUR NEW ROUTES THAT WOULD ADD
APPROXIMATELY 70 MILES TO THE SYSTEM.

DESIGNER
CHRIS FROETER
CHICAGO ILLINOIS

TYPOGRAPHIC SOURCE
IN-HOUSE

AGENCY
VSA PARTNERS,
INC.

CLIENT
LLINOIS STATE
TOLL HIGHWAY
AUTHORITY

PRINCIPAL TYPES
HELVETICA,
UNIVERS, AND
ZAPF DINGBATS

DIMENSIONS
8¹/₂ x 10 IN.
(21.6 x 25.4 CM)

GARY KOEPKE

ANNE-MARIE LOGAN

FLEMISH DRAWINGS IN THE AGE OF RUBENS
SELECTED WORKS FROM AMERICAN COLLECTIONS

DAVIS MUSEUM AND CULTURAL CENTER
Wellesley College

A typographic crisis — that is the state of design today. Not that I'm opposed to variety, but things seem to be getting out of hand. We all need to take a serious look at what is motivating our typography and why we choose to do it. This is why the book *Flemish Drawings in the Age of Rubens* and the graffiti on the towel dispenser in the men's room were the most impressive works of typography in this year's show. They both did the right thing for their particular subject matter.

The typography in *Flemish Drawings* was modern yet classical. It solved the problem and communicated the message properly. The production of the entire book was superb and the attention to detail was evident on every page. The typography was so well done and unassuming that not once did I think about the designer, until I realized that she hadn't imposed her ego all over the paintings and text. How thankful I was for that. It's something that seems to be missing from many of our typographic solutions these days. This constraint along with the attention to detail is why I consider it the best of show.

The exhibition Flemish Drawings in the Age of Rubens was the first to examine seventeenth-century Flemish draughtsmanship in over fifty years. In it unknown and recently attributed works were unveiled with new interpretations.

The exhibition catalog, inspired by late nineteenth- and early twentieth-century drawing books and folios, reinterprets these early publications. The oversize format, following the size and proportions of its antecedents, allows the drawings to be reproduced at a large scale, some to actual size. The book is bound to open flat to facilitate viewing the images. The paper is specially calendered, uncoated off-white stock that suggests the papers on which the drawings were originally executed. The red glorified spine employs a color traditional to the book arts; the uncovered bookbinder's board recalls folio covers; the debossed corners refer to leather-bound corners of historical books.

The typography is based on historical conventions which have been rethought, as the analyses of the drawings offer new interpretations. While alluding to the history of such folios, this publication embodies a rethinking of tradition.

DESIGNER
ANITA MEYER
BOSTON MASSACHUSETTS

EXHIBITION COORDINATOR
JUDITH HOOS FOX

PRINTER
**SNOECK—DUCAJO
+ ZOON**

CURATOR AND WRITER
ANNE-MARIE LOGAN

PRODUCTION COORDINATOR
SUSAN MCNALLY

TYPOGRAPHIC SOURCE
MOVEABLE TYPE INC.

STUDIO
PLUS DESIGN INC.

CLIENT
**DAVIS MUSEUM AND
CULTURAL CENTER**

PRINCIPAL TYPE
BERTHOLD WALBAUM

DIMENSIONS
**9⅞ × 14 IN.
(25.1 × 35.6 CM)**

SEVENTEENTH-CENTURY FLEMISH DRAWINGS

In the age of Rubens, Antwerp was the artistic center of the southern Netherlands, an area roughly equivalent to present-day Belgium. The court with the regents of the Spanish Netherlands, who were appointed by the Spanish king, the Archduke Albert of Austria (1559–1621) and Archduchess Isabella Clara Eugenia (1566–1655), daughter of Philip II, resided in Brussels. The division of the Netherlands began as early as 1579, when the seven northern provinces—dominated by Holland—formed the Union of Utrecht. Their independence from the southern or Spanish Netherlands was acknowledged only in 1609, at the time of the Twelve Years' Truce, and legalized with the Peace of Münster in 1648. The northern Netherlands became the independent Dutch Republic, or the United Provinces, where Protestantism in the form of Calvinism was predominant, while the southern Netherlands (often referred to—not quite correctly—as Flanders, one of the provinces) remained loyal to the Spanish king with Catholicism as the prevalent religion. Netherlandish art separated early in the seventeenth century into the Dutch school in the north and the Flemish school in the south. During the first half of the seventeenth century, the two Netherlands still had much in common, with artists moving back and forth; by mid-century, however, the northern Netherlands had become a dominant force in world trade and Amsterdam succeeded Antwerp as the artistic center.

The late sixteenth century was an economically trying time in the southern Netherlands. There was great devastation during the occupation by the Spanish army under Alessandro Farnese, ending with the fall of Antwerp in 1585. A former Calvinist stronghold, Antwerp lost about half of its citizens, who fled to neighboring Holland and Germany, among them a fairly large number of artists. Some prosperity reemerged, in particular, during the Twelve Years' Truce from 1609 until 1621. During this temporary peace, churches, monasteries, and public buildings in the southern Netherlands that had been devastated were restored and a number of new churches were built.

In both north and south, the prosperous middle class was instrumental in commissioning works of art. Differences in artistic trends in the south were stimulated by the aims of the Counter-Reformation to propagate the Catholic faith. In the northern Netherlands few paintings were found in churches, while in the south the introduction of large altarpieces was an important part of church decoration. In the Spanish Netherlands the churches became important patrons, supported by rich merchants, at times even by an entire city or town population. Guilds, as well as religious confraternities, were another rich source for commissions since both usually had their own chapels, often adorned with an altarpiece dedicated to their respective patron saint. A good example of this patronage is the guild of the Arquebusiers, which funded Rubens's DESCENT FROM THE CROSS (see under catalogue number 45). A factor contributing to the growth of the arts in the Spanish Netherlands was the religious fervor of the Jesuits (Society of Jesus) founded in 1540. The Society became a driving force in Antwerp with the building of a new church, consecrated in 1621. Rubens not only painted the ceiling decoration and the main altars for this Jesuit church, but also designed sculptural decorations and was involved in the design of the façade. The colleges of the Jesuits and of other religious orders

The David Byrne packaging succeeds both aesthetically and intellectually by combining elements of discovery, graphic analytical photography, a play on positive and negative spatial masses, and intriguing typographic manipulation.

Helvetica Regular (Helvetica Neue Roman), the most quiet of all modern faces, acts as the perfect vehicle for layering and patterning by giving this piece an interest beyond pure photographic expression. David Byrne's name on the front cover, with his last name in mirror reading backwards, serves as a metaphor for the portraiture of Byrne illustrated in the interior.

Each photograph, shot and printed with exacting detail, progressively takes the viewer into a closer examination of Byrne's body. What makes this photography memorable is that it achieves an investigative format without ever becoming voyeuristic.

Designed and printed in black and white, one's interest is further captured by moments of questioning as one discovers what body parts are being depicted. We literally and figuratively get to know David Byrne in this sophisticated example of conceptual design.

David wanted the "rawness" of his new CD to come through in my design for both the CD and the Special Package. I came up with this idea to take the rawness one more step—to "cut him open" and "peel back the layers" to more or less analyze him under a microscope. I felt that Jean Baptiste Mondino was the only one that could do that powerfully. I decided to create this 100-page book with a CD die-cut into the inside-front cover. At the time the Agfa Corporation had come to me to test a revolutionary new technology they were developing called Crystal-Raster (screenless printing that resembles photography because of its organic composition) and I convinced Warner Bros. Records to let me create the book using it. I designed the type as "DNA-like" structures to echo the scientific "techno" theme of the photos, while still keeping the "rawness" intact.

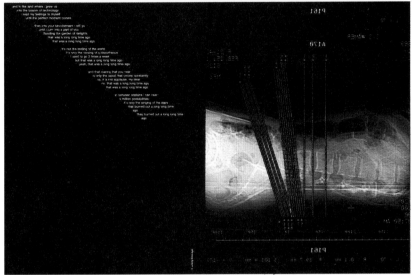

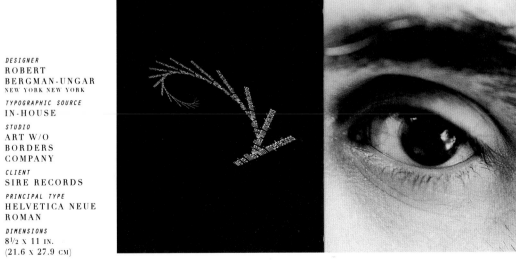

DESIGNER
ROBERT BERGMAN-UNGAR
NEW YORK NEW YORK

TYPOGRAPHIC SOURCE
IN-HOUSE

STUDIO
ART W/O BORDERS COMPANY

CLIENT
SIRE RECORDS

PRINCIPAL TYPE
HELVETICA NEUE ROMAN

DIMENSIONS
8¹/₂ x 11 IN. (21.6 x 27.9 CM)

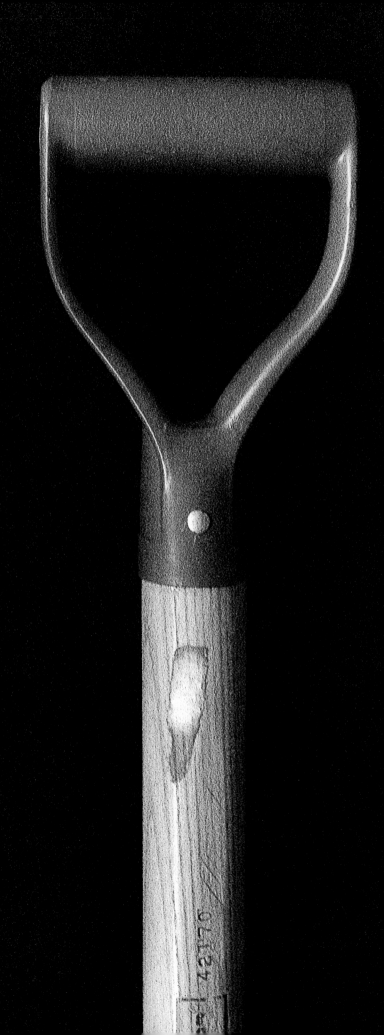

ENTRIES SELECTED FOR TYPOGRAPHIC EXCELLENCE

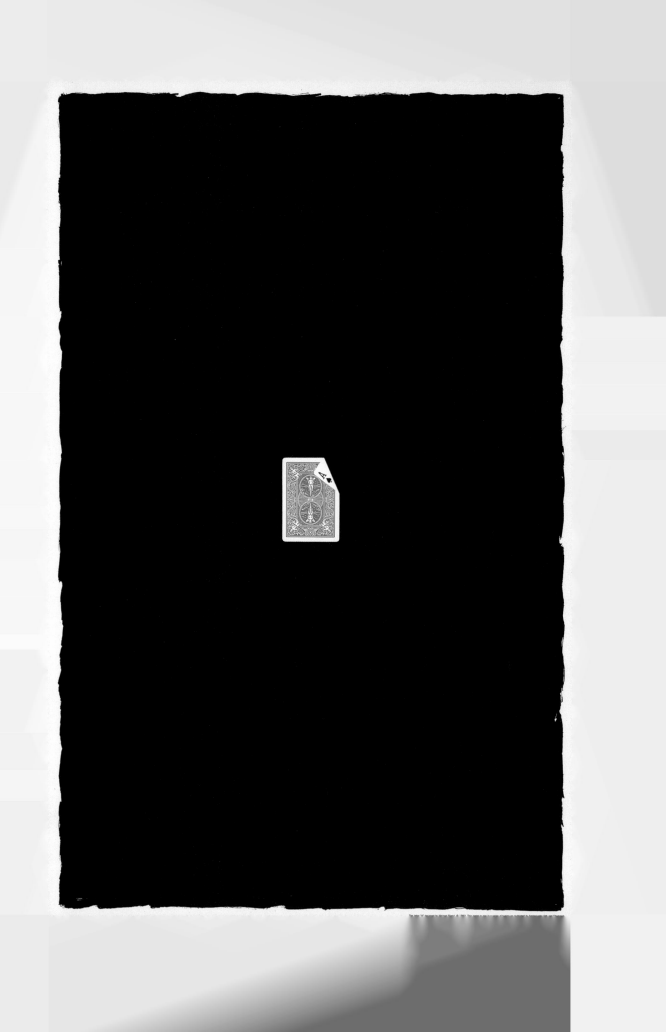

The letter "A" designed by Michael Bierut. © 1997. This poster is one in a series of posters produced by Ampersands Arts and Letters.

DESIGNER
XU WANG
GUANGZHOU CHINA

CALLIGRAPHER
KAN TAI-KEUNG

PHOTOGRAPHER
LEE KA-SIN
HONG KONG

TYPOGRAPHIC SOURCE
IN-HOUSE

STUDIO
SINO-WEST
DESIGN COMPANY

CLIENT
EXCHANGE
PUBLISH HOUSE

PRINCIPAL TYPE
HANDLETTERING

DESIGNERS
**TADASHI
MORISAKI,
MASAYUKI
YAMAMOTO,
TADANOBU
HARA, SHUN-
ICHI MIKI, AND
SARI TANIMURA**
TSUKUBA IBARAKI
JAPAN

ART DIRECTOR
**TADASHI
MORISAKI**
YOKOHAMA
KANAGAWA JAPAN

TYPOGRAPHIC SOURCE
IN-HOUSE

STUDIO
**FLYING RODENT
DESIGN**

CLIENT
**UNIVERSITY
OF TSUKUBA**

PRINCIPAL TYPES
**HEISEI-KAKU-
GOTHIC, GONA
DB, OCR-B,
AND CASLON**

ILLUSTRATOR
**NORIKO
SAGESAKA**

DIMENSIONS
**32 x 43 IN.
(81.3 x 109.2 CM)**

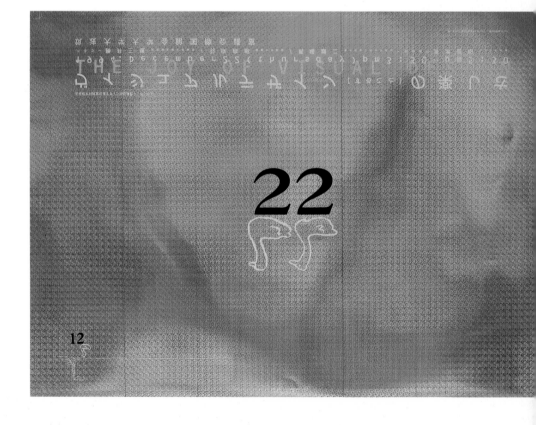

Baltimore Playwrights Festival

BY:

STEVE SCHUTZMAN

GHOSTS PLAY

ONE

This is not a home.

276-7837

Fells Point Corner Theatre

DESIGNER
PAUL SAHRE
BALTIMORE MARYL

TYPOGRAPHIC SOUR
IN-HOUSE

CLIENT
FELLS POINT
CORNER
THEATRE

PRINCIPAL TYPE
ADOBE
GARAMOND

DIMENSIONS
13½ × 20 IN.
(34.3 × 50.8 CM

Sahre

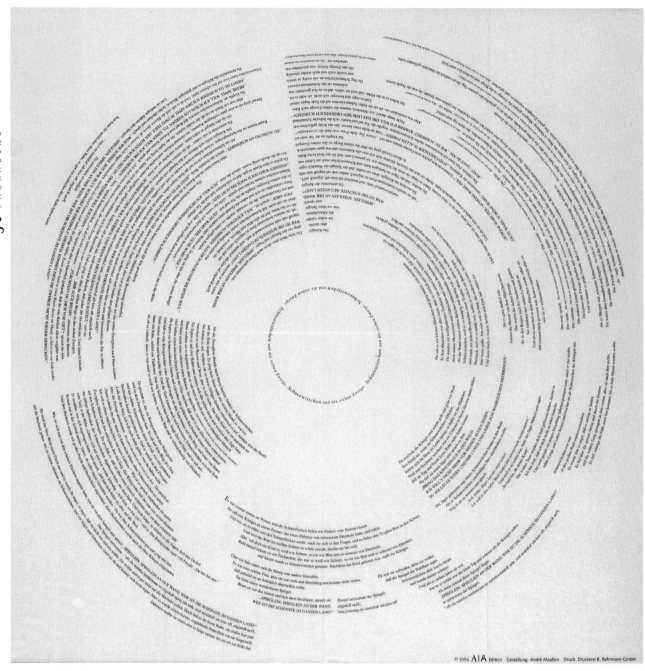

© 1994 AIA Edition Gestaltung: André Maaßen Druck: Druckerei B. Rehrmann GmbH

DESIGNER
ANDRÉ MAASSEN
WUPPERTAL GERMANY

TYPOGRAPHIC SOURCE
IN-HOUSE AND DRUCKEREI B. REHRMANN GMBH

STUDIO
ATELIER FÜR KOMMUNIKA-TIONSDESIGN MAASSEN/FRANKE

CLIENT
DRUCKEREI B. REHRMANN

PRINCIPAL TYPE
TIMES

DIMENSIONS
$17^{3}/_{4}$ x $17^{3}/_{4}$ IN. (45 x 45 CM)

DESIGNERS
INGO HAAK,
CHRISTIAN BOROS,
AND SYLVIA
ZÖLLER
WUPPERTAL GERMANY

TYPOGRAPHIC SOURCE
IN-HOUSE

AGENCY
BOROS
AGENTUR FÜR
KOMMUNIKATION

CLIENT
COMPUNET
COMPUTER AG

PRINCIPAL TYPE
UNIVERS

DIMENSIONS
11^{13}/$_{16}$ X 16^{1}/$_{2}$ IN.
(30 X 42 CM)

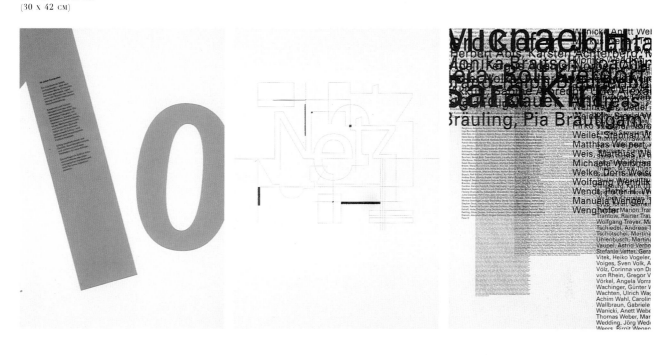

DESIGNER
DAN RICHARDS
BEAVERTON OREGON

LETTERER
DAN RICHARDS

TYPOGRAPHIC SOURCE
IN-HOUSE

STUDIO
NIKE, DESIGN

CLIENT
NIKE

DIMENSIONS
7 X 11 IN.
(17.8 X 27.9 CM)

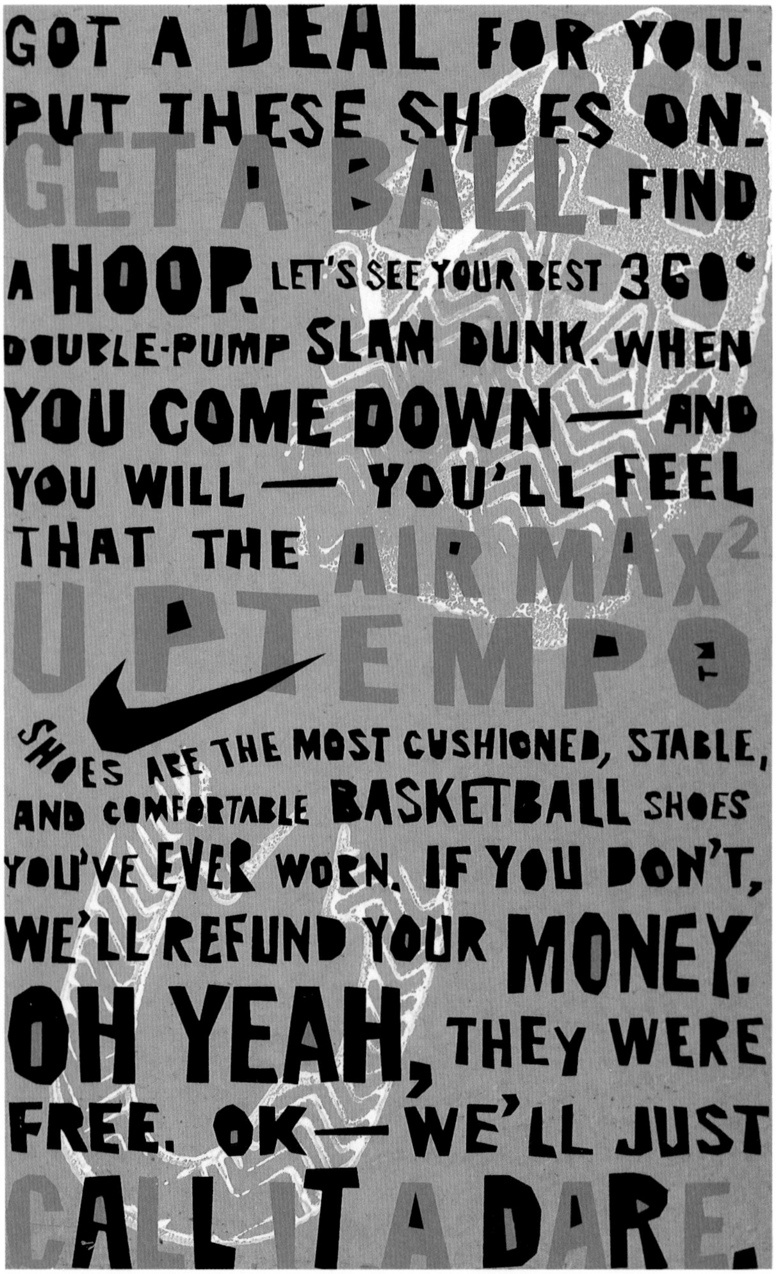

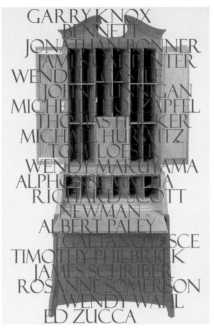

DESIGNERS
**MICHAEL BIERUT
AND ESTHER
BRIDAVSKY**
NEW YORK NEW YORK

TYPOGRAPHIC SOURCE
IN-HOUSE

STUDIO
**PENTAGRAM
DESIGN**

CLIENT
**PETER JOSEPH
GALLERY**

PRINCIPAL TYPES
**ADOBE GARAMOND,
FELIX, AND PEIGNOT
CONDENSED**

DIMENSIONS
**8 x 11¹⁄₂ IN.
(20.3 x 29.2 CM)**

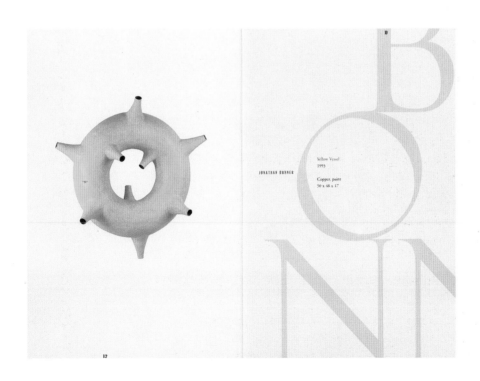

DESIGNERS
ZEMPAKU SUZUKI
MASAHIRO NAITO
AND NAHOKO
MOROOKA
SHINTOMI TOKYO JAPAN

LETTERER
YOICHI
HASHIKURA

ART DIRECTOR
JUN HARA AND
ZEMPAKU SUZUKI

PHOTOGRAPHER
TOSHIAKI
TAKEUCHI

TYPOGRAPHIC SOURCE
IN-HOUSE

AGENCY
AOI ADVERTISING
PROMOTION INC.

STUDIO
B•BI STUDIO INC.

CLIENT
SONY MUSIC
ENTERTAINMENT
INC.

PRINCIPAL TYPE
FRANKLIN GOTHIC

DIMENSIONS
$28^{2}/_{3}$ X $40^{9}/_{16}$ IN.
(72.8 X 103 CM)

POSTER

DESIGNER
UWE LOESCH
DÜSSELDORF GERMANY

TYPOGRAPHIC SOURCE
IN-HOUSE

CLIENT
ZANDERS
FEINPAPIERE AG

PRINCIPAL TYPE
FUTURA BOLD

DIMENSIONS
$4^{1}/_{8}$ X $8^{1}/_{4}$ IN.
(10.5 X 21 CM)
AND $7^{7}/_{8}$ X 11 IN.
(20 X 28 CM)

new album "AWAKE" 8.21 on sale

DESIGNER
PETER SMITH
LONDON ENGLAND

LETTERER
PETER SMITH

TYPOGRAPHIC SOURCE
IN-HOUSE

STUDIO
DIALOG LIMITED

CLIENT
DIALOG LIMITED

PRINCIPAL TYPE
NEWS GOTHIC

dialog

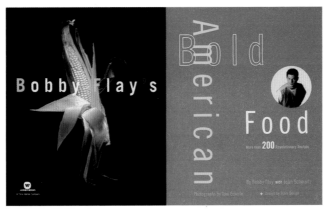

DESIGNERS
ADRIANE STARK
AND CHRISTINE
LICATA
NEW YORK NEW YORK

TYPOGRAPHIC SOURCE
IN-HOUSE

STUDIO
STARK DESIGN

CLIENT
WARNER BOOKS

PRINCIPAL TYPE
TRADE GOTHIC

DIMENSIONS
8¾ x 10¼ IN.
(22.2 x 26 CM)

DESIGNER
MICHAEL A.
BRALEY
SAN FRANCISCO
CALIFORNIA

TYPOGRAPHIC SOURCE
IN-HOUSE

AGENCY
STONE
YAMASHITA

CLIENT
STONE
YAMASHITA

PRINCIPAL TYPES
BAUER BODONI
AND WHIRLIGIG

DIMENSIONS
4¼ x 5½ IN.
(10.8 x 14 CM)

DESIGNERS
DAVID COVELL,
DAN SHARP, IAN
FACTOR, AND
KEITH BROWN
BURLINGTON VERMONT

ART DIRECTOR
DAVID COVELL

CREATIVE DIRECTOR
MICHAEL JAGER

TYPOGRAPHIC SOURCE
IN-HOUSE

STUDIO
JAGER DI PAOLA
KEMP DESIGN

CLIENT
BURTON
SNOWBOARDS

PRINCIPAL TYPES
AKZIDENZ
GROTESK,
CLARENDON,
COOPER BLACK,
FUTURA, AND
TRIXIE

DIMENSIONS
9½ x 12 IN.
(24.1 x 30.5 CM)

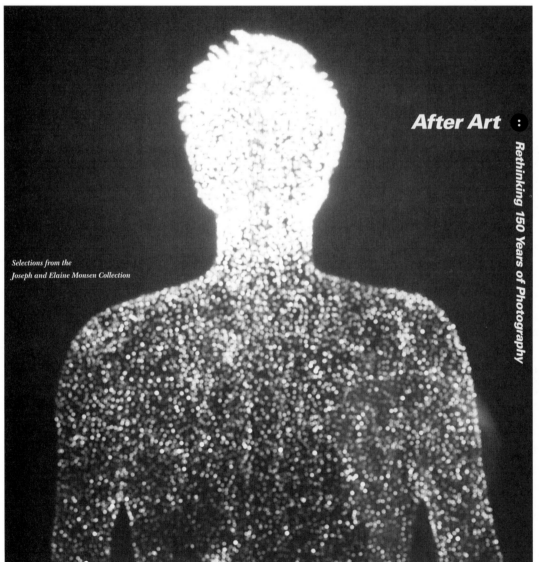

After Art :

Rethinking 150 Years of Photography

*Selections from the
Joseph and Elaine Monsen Collection*

DESIGNER
**DOUGLAS
WADDEN**
SEATTLE WASHINGTON

TYPOGRAPHIC SOURCE
**THOMAS AND
KENNEDY
TYPOGRAPHERS**

STUDIO
**DESIGN
COLLABORATIVE**

CLIENT
**HENRY ART
GALLERY**

PRINCIPAL TYPE
UNIVERS

DIMENSIONS
11¾ x 11¾ IN.
(29.9 x 29.9 CM)

DESIGNERS
NICHOLAS
LOWIE AND
SHERIDAN
LOWREY
VENICE CALIFORNIA

TYPOGRAPHIC SOURCE
IN-HOUSE

STUDIO
LOWIE/LOWREY
DESIGN

CLIENT
THE GETTY
CENTER FOR
THE HISTORY
OF ART AND
HUMANITIES

PRINCIPAL TYPES
BODONI,
HELVETICA,
GARAMOND,
GOUDY, AND
GROTESQUE

DIMENSIONS
6¹/₄ x 9 IN.
(15.9 x 22.9 CM)

Special Cases:

NATURAL

ANOMALIES

&
HISTORICAL
MONSTERS

The Getty Center

FOR THE HISTORY
OF ART AND THE

HUMANITIES

SEPTEMBER 24 – DECEMBER 17, 1994

PHOTOGRAPHS BY
MATTHEW ROLSTON

WHERE THE

ADAM HOROVITZ ▶

◀ MICHAEL DIAMOND

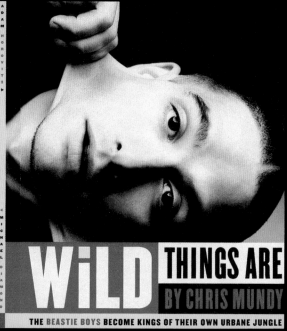

WILD THINGS ARE
BY CHRIS MUNDY

THE BEASTIE BOYS BECOME KINGS OF THEIR OWN URBANE JUNGLE

DESIGNERS
FRED
WOODWARD
AND GERALDINE
HESSLER
NEW YORK NEW YORK

ART DIRECTOR
FRED
WOODWARD

TYPOGRAPHIC SOURCE
IN-HOUSE

STUDIO
ROLLING STONE

CLIENT
ROLLING STONE

PRINCIPAL TYPE
CHAMPION
FAMILY OF
FACES

DIMENSIONS
12 x 20 IN. (30.5 x
50.8 CM)

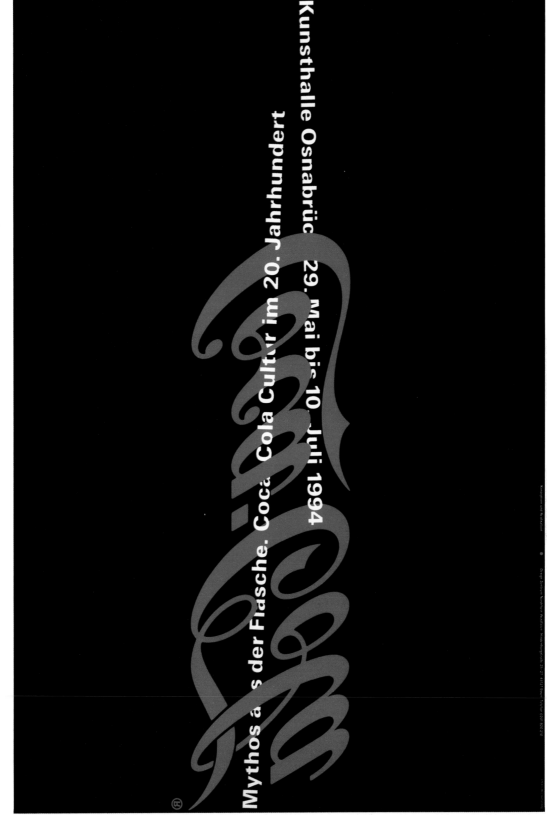

DESIGNER
UWE LOESCH
DÜSSELDORF GERMANY

TYPOGRAPHIC SOURCE
IN-HOUSE

CLIENT
DESIGN
ZENTRUM
NORDRHEIN
WESTFALEN

PRINCIPAL TYPE
UNIVERS BOLD

DIMENSIONS
33¹/₁₆ × 47⁷/₈ IN.
(84 × 119 CM)

DESIGNER
DAVID J. HWANG
HOLLYWOOD
CALIFORNIA

TYPOGRAPHIC SOURCE
IN-HOUSE

STUDIO
TWO HEADED
MONSTER

CLIENT
FOX SPORTS

PRINCIPAL TYPE
FRANKLIN
GOTHIC HEAVY

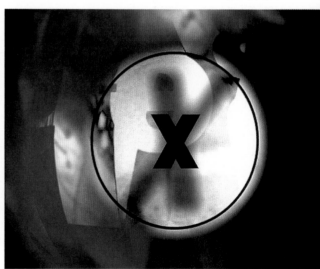

DESIGNER
DIRK WEBER
DÜSSELDORF GERMANY

TYPOGRAPHIC SOURCE
IN-HOUSE

STUDIO
**PROF. HELFRIED
HAGENBERG,
FACHBEREICH
DESIGN FH
DÜSSELDORF**

CLIENT
**FACHHOCHSCHULE
DÜSSELDORF**

PRINCIPAL TYPE
ITC OFFICINA

DIMENSIONS
**33 1/16 X 23 3/8 IN.
(84 X 59.4 CM)**

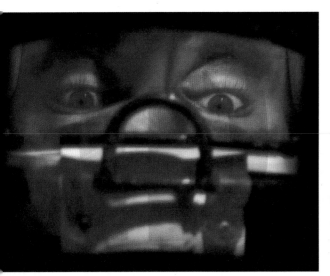

BOYS R US

Forget about slackers. Shut up about Winona forever. With their fourth album, *Ill Communication*, a street-level media empire, and a coheadlining spot on this summer's Lollapalooza, the once savage Beasties have proved to be the best and brightest of Generation X

By Alan Light

Photographs by Pierre Winther

Two-thirds of the Beastie Boys are sitting in a downtown Manhattan health food restaurant, sipping peppermint tea. The topic at hand is whether the Beasties—rap's original great white dopes—will ever be able to shake the image that skyrocketed them to stardom and infamy. Adam Yauch, better known as MCA, tries to capture the whole saga in one interview-friendly, sound-bite-quality moment.

"I'll give you a perfect story, something that happened only a couple of hours ago," says Yauch, whose recently dyed Winona hair may be the reason the kid in the Beastie Boys cap walked right past him outside the restaurant. "This is going to sum it all up journalistically for you—this is your shit right here.

"I went to the health food store to buy a juicer as a late Christmas present for my parents, so they can make carrot juice and stuff. I wanted to turn them on to it, because I got one and I'm really into it. So I go to the store in Brooklyn, kinda the B-boy health food spot. There's a couple of homeboys down there, and my man says, 'Yo, you're that dude from the Beastie Boys,' and I said,

'Yeah.' And the guy said, 'So, oh, I guess you guys don't drink 40s anymore?'"

Okay, so it's not that great a story; it's a little better in Yauch's deadpan, New-York-by-way-of-L.A. voice. But in a way, it really is all you need to know. Because what you might think about the Beastie Boys probably couldn't be further from the truth.

In 1986 the Beasties' debut album, *Licensed to Ill*, conquered the world in a haze of Budweiser spray, caged dancing girls, and cheap pot smoke. Fueled by the inescapable frat anthem "(You Gotta) Fight for Your Right (to Party)," it was the biggest-selling rap record ever, until M.C. Hammer came along. The group was also immediately dismissed as a one-hit novelty act—a sign of worse things to come, but certainly nothing to take too seriously.

It's now eight years later, and their new album, *Ill Communication*, further establishes the Beastie Boys as perhaps the most consistently innovative musicians to emerge out of hip hop. On top of which, the Beasties' other roles as businessmen, husbands, actors, snowboarders, clothing retailers, activists,

SO WHAT CH
The Beastie Boys—from left, Mike Diamond,
Adam Horovitz, Adam Yauch. MCA—are a link
line between the worlds of hip hop and alter...

DESIGNERS
GARY KOEPKE
AND DIDDO
RAMM
NEW YORK NEW YORK

TYPOGRAPHIC SOURCE
IN-HOUSE

STUDIO
VIBE MAGAZINE

CLIENT
VIBE MAGAZINE

PRINCIPAL TYPES
VIBRATION
GOTHIC AND
HELVETICA
BLACK

DIMENSIONS
12 x 20 IN.
(30.5 x 50.8 CM)

DESIGNER
DIDDO RAMM
NEW YORK NEW YORK
TYPOGRAPHIC SOURCE
IN-HOUSE
STUDIO
VIBE MAGAZINE
CLIENT
VIBE MAGAZINE
PRINCIPAL TYPE
VIBRATION
GOTHIC
DIMENSIONS
12 x 20 IN.
(30.5 x 50.8 CM)

Something is buzzing in Long Beach. Warren G welcomes you to the G funk era. By Cheo H. Coker

NOTHING BUT A G THANG

AS CASEY SIEMASZKO EXPLAINS six minutes into the movie *Young Guns*, regulation is no occupation for the squeamish. "You can't be any geek off the street," he says with a haughty air of defiance now immortalized in a

V I B E 73

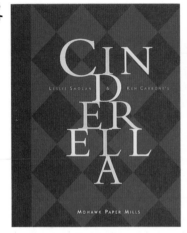

all
work I'm exhausted.

no
play

after
midnight

I rush past shocked ushers and fairly leap into the vehicle.

DESIGNERS
LESLIE
SMOLAN,
KEN CARBONE,
AND
CARLA MILLER
NEW YORK NEW YORK

TYPOGRAPHIC SOURCE
IN-HOUSE

STUDIO
CARBONE
SMOLAN
ASSOCIATES

CLIENT
MOHAWK PAPER
MILLS, INC.

PRINCIPAL TYPES
ADOBE BEMBO,
MONOTYPE
BEMBO,
BITSTREAM
GEOMETRIC 415

DIMENSIONS
9¾ x 12 IN.
(24.8 x 30.5 CM)

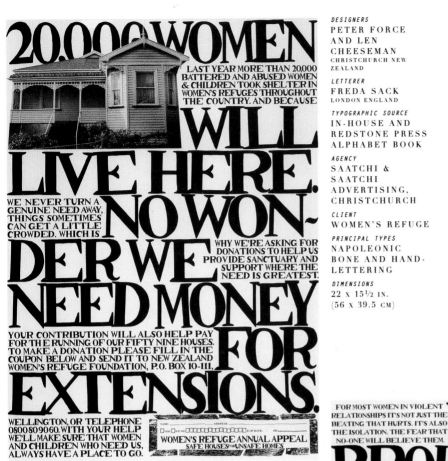

DESIGNERS
PETER FORCE
AND LEN
CHEESEMAN
CHRISTCHURCH NEW
ZEALAND

LETTERER
FREDA SACK
LONDON ENGLAND

TYPOGRAPHIC SOURCE
IN-HOUSE AND
REDSTONE PRESS
ALPHABET BOOK

AGENCY
SAATCHI &
SAATCHI
ADVERTISING,
CHRISTCHURCH

CLIENT
WOMEN'S REFUGE

PRINCIPAL TYPES
NAPOLEONIC
BONE AND HAND-
LETTERING

DIMENSIONS
22 x 15½ IN.
(56 x 39.5 CM)

DESIGNERS
PETER FORCE
AND LEN
CHEESEMAN
CHRISTCHURCH NEW
ZEALAND

LETTERER
FREDA SACK
LONDON ENGLAND

TYPOGRAPHIC SOURCE
IN-HOUSE AND
REDSTONE PRESS
ALPHABET BOOK

AGENCY
SAATCHI &
SAATCHI
ADVERTISING,
CHRISTCHURCH

CLIENT
WOMEN'S REFUGE

PRINCIPAL TYPES
NAPOLEONIC
BONE AND HAND-
LETTERING

DIMENSIONS
22 x 15½ IN.
(56 x 39.5 CM)

cyclops

s albert

watson

MARRAKESH

MANSOUR EDDAHBI

MOROCCO FEBRUARY

OUARZAZATE   WARS   ZBEL SARHO

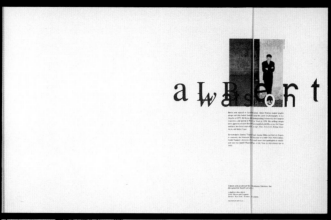

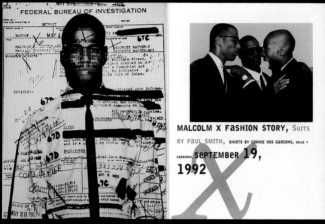

DESIGNER
DAVID CARSON
SAN DIEGO CALIFORNIA

TYPOGRAPHIC SOURCE
IN-HOUSE

STUDIO
DAVID CARSON
DESIGN

CLIENT
CALLAWAY
EDITIONS, INC.

PRINCIPAL TYPES
INDUSTRY SANS,
CANADIAN
PHOTOGRAPHER,
TIMES, CORNWALL,
AND ORATOR

DIMENSIONS
14¼ x 11¼ in.
(36.2 x 28.6 cm)

DESIGNERS
JILLY SIMONS,
DAVID SHIELDS,
AND SUSAN
CARLSON
CHICAGO ILLINOIS

WRITER
CHUCK CARLSON

TYPOGRAPHIC SOURCE
IN-HOUSE

STUDIO
CONCRETE

CLIENT
TONY STONE
IMAGES

PRINCIPAL TYPES
GARAMOND
AND AVENIR

DIMENSIONS
4 3/8 X 6 1/8 IN.
(11.7 X 15.5 CM)

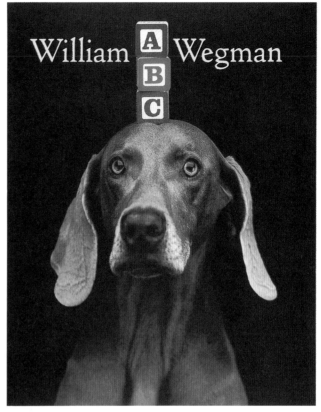

Batty has a sock on her nose.
She thinks she looks like an

ELEPHANT.

DESIGNER
GARY TOOTH
NEW YORK NEW YORK

CREATIVE DIRECTOR
STEPHEN DOYLE

TYPOGRAPHIC SOURCE
IN-HOUSE

STUDIO
DRENTTEL DOYLE
PARTNERS

CLIENT
HYPERION BOOKS
FOR CHILDREN

PRINCIPAL TYPES
WEIMARANER AND
CLOISTER

DIMENSIONS
8¹/₂ X 11 IN.
(21.6 X 27.9 CM)

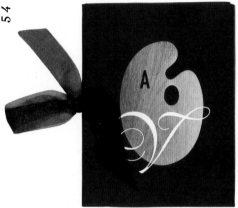

Board of Trustees

Steve Hearne *President*, Katherine Boone *Vice President*
Jeanne Jaffee *Vice President*, Sittie Fischer *Secretary*
Betty Schermer *Treasurer*, Larry Hubbard *National Council Chair*
Barbara Berger, Ruth Brown, Carol Chanin, Ron Dalby
Marian Lyeth Davis, Nanette Finger, Larry Hubbard,
Melissa Jaffee, Pamela Joseph, Betty Moore, Mary Patton,
Shazi Press, Bob Schultz, Evelyn Siegel, Jeff Thinnes

Lifetime Trustees

Betsy Chaffin, Tom Hubbard, Harriet Kelly
Lee Lyon, Kathy Smith, Marge Stein

Special Advisor

Floyd Mann

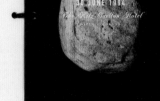

30 JUNE 1994
The Ritz-Carlton Hotel

DESIGNERS
JAMES KOVAL AND
JENNIFFER WIESS
CHICAGO ILLINOIS

TYPOGRAPHIC SOURCE
IN-HOUSE

DESIGN FIRM
VSA PARTNERS,
INC.

CLIENT
ANDERSON
RANCH, ASPEN,
COLORADO

PRINCIPAL TYPES
POPPI-RESIDENZ,
GARAMOND NO. 3,
AND DIN
ENGSCHRIFT

DIMENSIONS
INVITATION: 4³/₄ x 6 IN.
(12.1 x 15.2 CM)
POSTER: 18 x 21¹/₂ IN.
(45.7 x 54.6 CM)

DESIGNER
CHRISTOPHER
DAVIS
NEW YORK NEW YORK

TYPOGRAPHIC SOURCE
IN-HOUSE

AGENCY
MTV OFF-AIR
CREATIVE

CLIENT
MTV:MUSIC
TELEVISION

PRINCIPAL TYPES
SCRIPT MT
BOLD, AKZIDENZ
GROTESK
SUPER, AND
FOUND WOOD
TYPE

DIMENSIONS
10 x 13 IN.
(25.4 x 33 CM)
STATIONERY
ENVELOPE

MTV NETWORKS. ALL RIGHTS RESERVED

MTV NETWORKS. ALL RIGHTS RESERVED

MTV

Video Music Awards

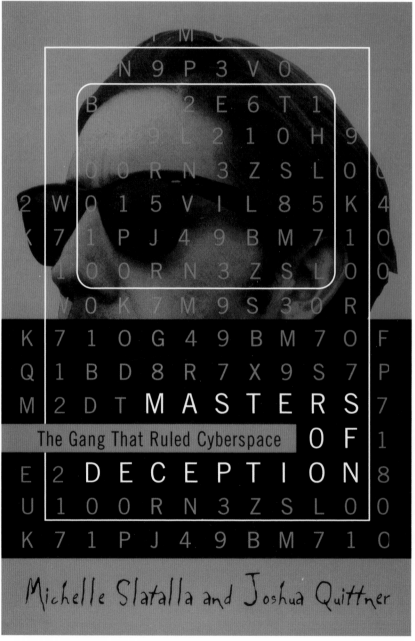

DESIGNER
ROBERTO DE VICQ
DE CUMPTICH
NEW YORK NEW YORK
TYPOGRAPHIC SOURCE
IN-HOUSE
CLIENT
HARPERCOLLINS/
NEW YORK
PRINCIPAL TYPES
TRADE GOTHIC
AND ROUGFHOUSE
DIMENSIONS
6¹/₂ x 9¹/₂ IN.
(16.5 x 24.1 CM)

DESIGNER
NEAL ASHBY
WASHINGTON D.C.

LETTERER
NEAL ASHBY

TYPOGRAPHIC SOURCE
IN-HOUSE

AGENCY
RECORDING
INDUSTRY
ASSOCIATION
OF AMERICA

CLIENT
RECORDING
INDUSTRY
ASSOCIATION OF
AMERICA

PRINCIPAL TYPES
NEW BASKERVILLE
AND MATRIX

DIMENSIONS
8¹/₂ x 13 IN.
(21.6 x 33 CM)

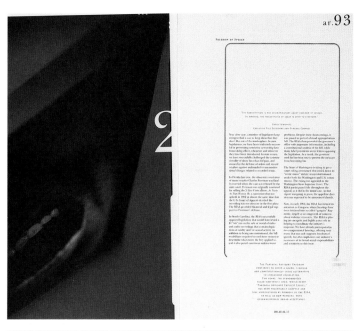

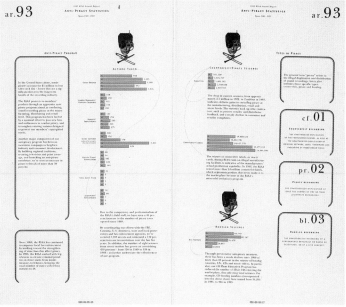

DESIGNERS
HENRICH
FÖRSTER, JAN
KRUSE, WIEBKE
OESER, YVONNE
FEIN, BIRKE
KÜSZER, ARMIN
ILLION,
STEFFEN
KLOPPROGGE,
RENA
CHRYSSIKOPOU-
LOU, SIBYLLE
REICHELT, AND
MAIKE
TRUSCHKOWSKI
KASSEL GERMANY

TYPOGRAPHIC SOURCE
IN-HOUSE

STUDIO
UNIVERSITÄT
GH KASSEL,
LEHRBEREICH
PROF. CHRISTOF
GASSNER

CLIENT
UNIVERSITÄT
GH KASSEL

PRINCIPAL TYPE
VARIOUS

DIMENSIONS
8⁶/₁₃ x 11 IN.
(21.5 x 28 CM)

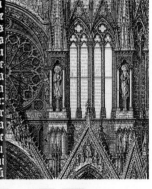

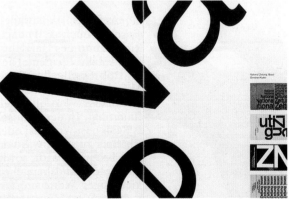

DESIGNER
DAVID CARSON
SAN DIEGO CALIFORNIA

TYPOGRAPHIC SOURCE
IN·HOUSE

STUDIO
DAVID CARSON
DESIGN

CLIENT
RAY GUN

PRINCIPAL TYPE
TEENAGER AND
INSIDE OUT

DIMENSIONS
10 x 12 IN.
(25.4 x 30.5 CM)

DESIGNERS
CHIP KIDD
AND BARBARA
DeWILDE
NEW YORK NEW YORK

TYPOGRAPHIC SOURCE
IN-HOUSE

STUDIO
CHIP KIDD
DESIGN

CLIENT
ALFRED A.
KNOPF, INC.

PRINCIPAL TYPE
BERNHARD
MODERN
AND FUTURA

DIMENSIONS
$14^{1}/_{2}$ X $9^{1}/_{2}$ IN.
(36.9 X 24.1 CM)

THE OLD

Moderns

ESSAYS ON
LITERATURE AND THEORY

DENIS DONOGHUE

DESIGNER
XU WANG
GUANGZHOU CHINA

TYPOGRAPHIC SOURCE
IN-HOUSE

STUDIO
SINO-WEST
DESIGN
COMPANY

CLIENT
TAIWAN IMAGE
POSTER DESIGN
ASSOCIATION

PRINCIPAL TYPE
HELVETICA

DIMENSIONS
23⅝ x 33½ IN.
(60 x 85 CM)

DESIGNER
LISA OVERTON
NEW YORK NEW YORK

TYPOGRAPHIC SOURCE
IN-HOUSE

STUDIO
BIG PINK, INC.

CLIENT
VH-1

PRINCIPAL TYPES
HELVETICA
ULTRA
COMPRESSED
AND BLUR

DESIGNERS
HANS DIETER
REICHERT, BRIAN
CUNNINGHAM,
MALCOLM
GARRETT,
STEPHANIE
GRANGER, AND
DEAN PAVITT
EAST MALLING KENT
ENGLAND

ART DIRECTOR
HANS DIETER
REICHERT

CREATIVE DIRECTOR
HANS DIETER
REICHERT

PHOTOGRAPHER
HDR DESIGN
AND IAN TEH

TYPOGRAPHIC SOURCE
IN-HOUSE

STUDIO
HDR DESIGN

CLIENT
ESSELTE
LETRASET

PRINCIPAL TYPE
CHARLOTTE SANS

EDITOR
MIKE DAINES

EDITORAL ADVISORY BOARD
MARTIN ASHLEY,
COLIN BRIGNALL,
MIKE DAINES,
DAVID ELLIS,
CHRIS GRAY, AND
HANS DIETER
REICHERT

DIMENSIONS
9⅝ × 13¼ IN.
(24.5 × 34.7 CM)

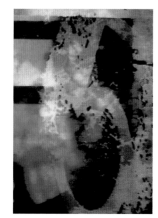

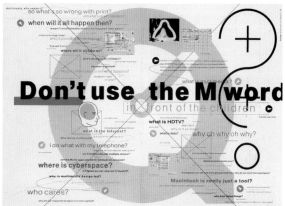

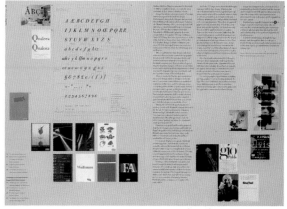

DESIGNER
TODD
WATERBURY
PORTLAND OREGON

LETTERER
TODD
WATERBURY

WRITER
PETER WEGNER

TYPOGRAPHIC SOURCE
IN-HOUSE

AGENCY
WIEDEN &
KENNEDY

CLIENT
THE COCA-COLA
COMPANY

PRINCIPAL TYPES
NEWS GOTHIC,
COURIER,
ALTERNATE
GOTHIC, AND
HANDLETTERING

DESIGNER
TODD
WATERBURY
PORTLAND OREGON

LETTERER
TODD
WATERBURY

WRITER
PETER WEGNER

TYPOGRAPHIC SOURCE
IN-HOUSE

AGENCY
WIEDEN &
KENNEDY

CLIENT
THE COCA-COLA
COMPANY

PRINCIPAL TYPES
NEWS GOTHIC,
COURIER,
ALTERNATE
GOTHIC, AND
HANDLETTERING

THE ROLLING STONE COMPUTER ISSUE

CYBER NATION

PAUL ALLEN, SHY BILLIONAIRE, TRIES TO ROCK THE I-WAY

MR. MICROSOFTEE

BY KIT BOSS

PAUL ALLEN is ripping through "Purple Haze," and to say he sounds like a million bucks would be to misplace the decimal point. ➤ ALLEN PLAYS guitar in a Seattle pickup group named the Threads, which others have called the World's Most Expensive Garage Band. Allen – the co-founder of the world's largest software company, Microsoft; majority owner of the world's largest concert-ticket distributor, Ticketmaster; die-hard Jimi Hendrix fan – is No. 11 on the Forbes list of the 400 richest Americans. His net worth is $3.9 billion. More

DESIGNER
LEE BEARSON
NEW YORK NEW YORK
ART DIRECTOR
FRED
WOODWARD
TYPOGRAPHIC SOURCE
IN-HOUSE
PRINCIPAL TYPE
CHAMPION
FAMILY OF
FACES
DIMENSIONS
10 x 12 IN.
(25.4 x 30.5 CM)

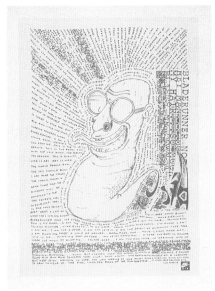

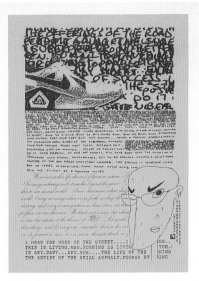

DESIGNERS
THESEUS CHAN
AND JIM AITCHISON
SINGAPORE

LETTERER
THESEUS CHAN

TYPOGRAPHIC SOURCE
IN-HOUSE

AGENCY
CHAN/AITCHISON
PARTNERSHIP

CLIENT
D CORNER

PRINCIPAL TYPES
HANDLETTERING
AND FAXED
TYPEWRITER COPY

ILLUSTRATOR
THESEUS CHAN

DIMENSIONS
22 x 15¾ IN. (56 x 40 CM)

DESIGNERS
MAELIN LEVINE,
AMY LEVINE,
AND JASON
JANUS
SAN DIEGO CALIFORNIA

TYPOGRAPHIC SOURCE
IN-HOUSE

STUDIO
VISUAL ASYLUM

CLIENT
VISUAL ASYLUM

PRINCIPAL TYPES
CITY, MONA
LISA, MATA,
BIRCH, AND
COPPERPLATE
GOTHIC

DIMENSIONS
5 × 2½ IN.
(12.7 × 6.4 CM)

DESIGNER
GERALDINE
HESSLER
NEW YORK NEW YORK

ART DIRECTOR
FRED
WOODWARD

TYPOGRAPHIC SOURCE
IN-HOUSE

STUDIO
ROLLING STONE

CLIENT
ROLLING STONE

PRINCIPAL TYPE
CHAMPION

DIMENSIONS
12 × 20 IN.
(30.5 × 50.8 CM)

SMASHING PUMPKINS

BY CHRIS MUNDY

ROLLING STONE, APRIL 21, 1994

ALL PUMPED UP: JIMMY CHAMBERLIN, JAMES IHA, BILLY CORGAN AND D'ARCY (FROM LEFT)

PHOTOGRAPHS BY CLEM LUCHFORD

OUTSIDE

THE BOX

Central Resource Group

19

Annual   Report

93

DESIGNERS
STEVE PATTEE
AND KELLY
STILES
DES MOINES IOWA

TYPOGRAPHIC SOURCE
IN-HOUSE

AGENCY
MIKE CONDON
INC.

STUDIO
PATTEE DESIGN

CLIENT
CENTRAL
RESOURCE
GROUP

PRINCIPAL TYPES
GARAMOND AND
20TH CENTURY
ULTRA BOLD

DIMENSIONS
8 x 11 IN.
(20.3 x 27.9 CM)

DESIGNER
GARY KOEPKE
MAGNOLIA
MASSACHUSETTS

TYPOGRAPHIC SOURCE
IN-HOUSE

STUDIO
**KOEPKE
INTERNATIONAL,
LTD.**

CLIENT
CHIEMSEE

PRINCIPAL TYPES
**SABON AND
HELVETICA**

DIMENSIONS
9 x 11½ IN.
(22.9 x 29.2 CM)

1 2 3 4 5 6 7

Um, Dois, Três: Matheus Rolston Essay. / Um, Dois e Três: Matheus; 7 Pictures/7 Imagens Editoriais. / 7 Pictures/7 Imagens / Um,

Foto: Matheus Rolston para/for: Editorial

DESIGNER
OSWALDO
MIRANDA
(MIRAN)
CURITABA PR BRAZIL

TYPOGRAPHIC SOURCE
FOTOLASER/
FONTE
FOTOCOMP.

STUDIO
CASA DE IDÉIAS

CLIENT
ADD PUBLISHER

PRINCIPAL TYPE
BODONI

DIMENSIONS
11⁷⁄₈ x 16¹³⁄₁₆ IN.
(30 x 43 CM)

DESIGNER
SUSAN SILTON
LOS ANGELES
CALIFORNIA

TYPOGRAPHIC SOURCE
IN-HOUSE

STUDIO
**SOS, LOS
ANGELES**

CLIENT
**SANTA MONICA
MUSEUM OF ART**

PRINCIPAL TYPE
VARIOUS

DIMENSIONS
**8 × 12 IN.
(20.3 × 30.5 CM)**

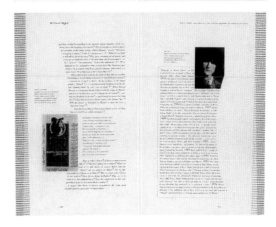

CARSON

florida

AIGA JACK-
SONVILLE+MIAMI,
AND SIMPSON
PAPER
P   R   E
S   E   N
T
JACKSONVILLE
JANUARY 25
MIAMI
JANUARY 26
END OF PRINT TOUR '95

DESIGNER
DAVID CARSON
SAN DIEGO CALIFORNIA

TYPOGRAPHIC SOURCE
IN-HOUSE

STUDIO
DAVID CARSON
DESIGN

CLIENT
AMERICAN
INSTITUTE OF
GRAPHIC ARTS/
MIAMI CHAPTER

PRINCIPAL TYPE
DIN
ENGSCHRIFT

DIMENSIONS
22 x 24 IN.
(55.9 x 61 CM)
POSTER

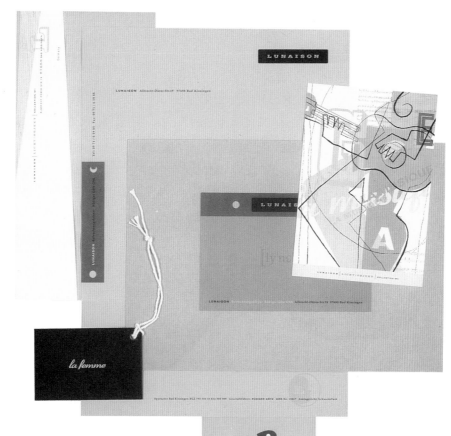

DESIGNER
RÜDIGER GÖTZ
HAMBURG GERMANY

LETTERER
RÜDIGER GÖTZ

TYPOGRAPHIC SOURCE
IN-HOUSE

STUDIO
FACTOR DESIGN

CLIENT
LUNAISON GBR

PRINCIPAL TYPES
PALATINO
AND HAND-
LETTERING

DIMENSIONS
VARIOUS

The next ten pages are devoted to the work of some young designers from the UK, Germany and the USA. The focus on young design has never been sharper. The 1980s saw the two types of graphic design organisation growing in parallel. The established groups working for corporate or mainstream clients sought to grow larger and more businesslike. It seemed for a while, in the UK, that management consultancy would outweigh creativity.

The rapid expansion of music and youth culture promotion created real budgets which could be used by the smaller, usually younger, newer groups. New magazines aimed at the young allowed and encouraged experiment; the whole process spawning images, styles and some design personalities, which spilled into the graphic design being created for more serious clients. To a large extent the recession has stopped some of the larger groups in their tracks, whilst low budget design has boomed.

Music and cultural clients allow the young designer to gain a foothold; widely distributed magazines cement the position of some as style leaders. And, of course, the independent designers, cooperatives and small groups embraced computer imagery first and have created a movement in techno-type and techno-typography which cannot be ignored.

The energy alone in much of the work can be seductive. It is worth remembering, though, that we are not necessarily getting a sneak preview of how all graphic design will be in a few years time. But while we are not trying to find a typographic pattern for the future there is some influential work in this collection.

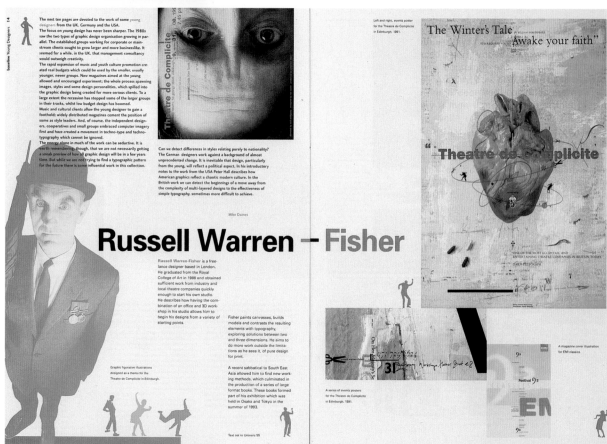

Can we detect differences in styles relating purely to nationality? The German designers work against a background of almost unprecedented change. It is inevitable that design, particularly from the young, will reflect a political aspect. In his introductory notes to the work from the USA Peter Hall describes how American graphics reflect a chaotic modern culture. In the British work we can detect the beginnings of a move away from the complexity of multi-layered designs to the effectiveness of simple typography, sometimes more difficult to achieve.

Mike Daines

Russell Warren – Fisher

Russell Warren-Fisher is a freelance designer based in London. He graduated from the Royal College of Art in 1988 and obtained sufficient work from industry and local theatre companies quickly enough to start his own studio. He describes how having the combination of an office and 3D workshop in his studio allows him to begin his designs from a variety of starting points.

Fisher paints canvasses, builds models and contrasts the resulting elements with typography, exploring solutions between two and three dimensions. He aims to do more work outside the limitations as he sees it, of pure design for print.

A recent sabbatical to South East Asia allowed him to find new working methods, which culminated in the production of a series of large format books. These books formed part of his exhibition which was held in Osaka and Tokyo in the summer of 1993.

Graphic figurative illustrations designed as a theme for the Theatre de Complicite in Edinburgh.

A series of events posters for the Theatre de Complicite in Edinburgh, 1991.

A magazine cover illustration for EMI classics.

Text set in Univers 55

DESIGNER
HANS DIETER
REICHERT
EAST MALLING KENT
ENGLAND

ASSISTANT DESIGNER
BRIAN
CUNNINGHAM

ART DIRECTOR
HANS DIETER
REICHERT

PHOTOGRAPHER
HDR DESIGN
AND EVERALD
WILLIAMS

EDITOR
MIKE DAINES

TYPOGRAPHIC SOURCE
IN-HOUSE

STUDIO
HDR DESIGN

CLIENT
ESSELTE
LETRASET

PRINCIPAL TYPE
CHARLOTTE
SANS

DIMENSIONS
9⅝ x 13¼ IN.
(24.5 x 33.7 CM)

DESIGNERS
CHERI DORR
AND
SUSANNA KO
NEW YORK NEW YORK

TYPOGRAPHIC SOURCES
IN-HOUSE
AND KENNEDY
YOUNG

AGENCY
VH-1

CLIENT
VH-1

PRINCIPAL TYPE
NEWS GOTHIC

DIMENSIONS
9 x 12 IN.
(22.9 x 30.5 CM)

DESIGNER
DIDDO RAMM
NEW YORK NEW YORK

TYPOGRAPHIC SOURCE
IN-HOUSE

STUDIO
VIBE MAGAZINE

CLIENT
VIBE MAGAZINE

PRINCIPAL TYPES
**BERTHOLD
GARAMOND AND
VIBRATION
GOTHIC**

DIMENSIONS
12 x 20 IN.
(30.5 x 50.8 CM)

DESIGNER
UWE LOESCH
DÜSSELDORF GERMANY

TYPOGRAPHIC SOURCE
IN-HOUSE

CLIENT
**LE MOUVEMENT
DE LA PAIX,
PARIS**

PRINCIPAL TYPE
DIN ENGSCHRIFT

DIMENSIONS
46⁷/₈ x 66¹/₈ IN.
(119 x 168 CM)

POSTER

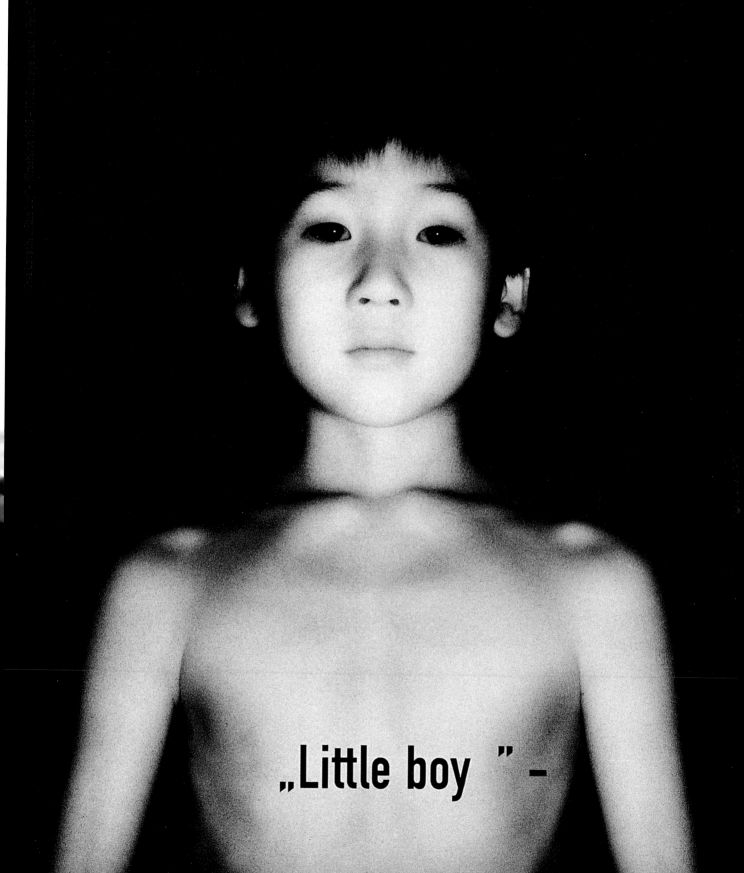

„Little boy " –

DESIGNER
JOHN VAN DYKE
SEATTLE WASHINGTON

TYPOGRAPHIC SOURCE
IN-HOUSE

STUDIO
VAN DYKE
COMPANY

CLIENT
AMERICAN
INSTITUTE OF
GRAPHIC
ARTS/SEATTLE

PRINCIPAL TYPES
BELUCIAN
BOOK, COOPER
BLACK, AND
OCR-B

DIMENSIONS
11 x 17 IN.
(27.9 x 43.2 CM)

DESIGNERS
JOHN VAN-DYKE
AND
DAVE MASON
SEATTLE WASHINGTON

TYPOGRAPHIC SOURCE
IN-HOUSE

STUDIO
A DESIGN
COLLABORATIVE

CLIENT
BC TELECOM

PRINCIPAL TYPES
SABON AND
FUTURA

DIMENSIONS
9 x 12 IN.
(22.9 x 30.5 CM)
ANNUAL
REPORT

DESIGNERS
RÜDIGER GÖTZ
AND JOHANNES
ERLER
HAMBURG GERMANY

LETTERERS
RÜDIGER GÖTZ
AND
OLAF STEIN

ART DIRECTOR
RÜDIGER GÖTZ

TYPOGRAPHIC SOURCE
IN-HOUSE

STUDIO
FACTOR DESIGN

CLIENT
FACTOR DESIGN

PRINCIPAL TYPES
SACKERS
GOTHIC AND
ALTERNATE
GOTHIC

DIMENSIONS
VARIOUS

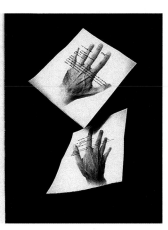

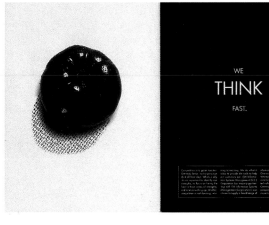

WE
MAKE
it
HAPPEN.

WE
THINK
FAST.

DESIGNERS
WOODY PIRTLE
AND IVETTE
MONTES DE OCA
NEW YORK NEW YORK

CALLIGRAPHER
WOODY PIRTLE

TYPOGRAPHIC SOURCE
IN-HOUSE

STUDIO
PENTAGRAM
DESIGN

CLIENT
AMERICAN
INSTITUTE OF
GRAPHIC ARTS

PRINCIPAL TYPE
SQUARE SLAB

DIMENSIONS
24 x 35½ IN.
(61 x 90.2 CM)

DESIGNER
NEIL POWELL
MINNEAPOLIS MINNESOTA

LETTERER
NEIL POWELL

TYPOGRAPHIC SOURCE
IN-HOUSE

STUDIO
DUFFY DESIGN

CLIENT
GRAPHIC
COMMUNCIATION
SOCIETY OF
OKLAHOMA

PRINCIPAL TYPES
HANDLETTERING
AND CUT-OUT
TYPE

DIMENSIONS
24 x 36 IN.
(61 x 91.4 CM)

POSTER

MINNEAPOLIS

DAY by DAY

BIG INDUSTRY

GET

A

JOB

POWELL, Neil

NEIL WHO?

they say merrily

rousing dance

gypsy rhythms

rollicking score

thrillingly colorful

most sublime   creations   **duffy**

magnificent

AFTER HOURS,

A.

high-wire

LONGER LASTING

things to come

TIK

career

TOK

An important break-through

CREATE

BLAST

REWARD

neil powell | duffy, inc.

get job. do a good job. keep job. sometimes easier said than done. but, if successful the rewards can be endless. neil powell will talk about how he went from an unemployed graduate to senior designer

at one of the country's top design firms, duffy, inc. and how his work in brand and corporate identity for such clients as the coca cola company, wieland furniture, and the stroh brewery

company is paving a critical path in his design career. presented by the graphic communication society of oklahoma. city arts center april 21, 1994.

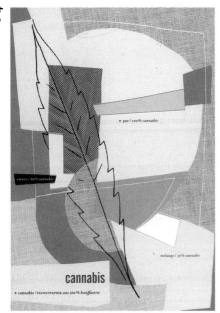

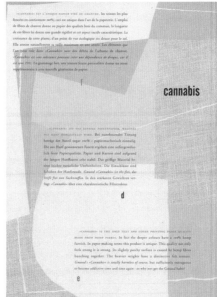

DESIGNER
RÜDIGER GÖTZ
HAMBURG GERMANY

TYPOGRAPHIC SOURCE
IN-HOUSE

STUDIO
FACTOR DESIGN

CLIENT
**PAPIERMÜHLE
GMUND**

PRINCIPAL TYPES
**GARAMOND
AND ALTERNATE
GOTHIC**

DIMENSIONS
VARIOUS

WHEN YOU BRING A BROWN
PAPER BAG OF COFFEE
HOME FROM THE MARKET,
THE STRONG FRAGRANCE
OF DARK-ROASTED BEANS
ACCOMPANIES YOU EVERY-
WHERE YOU GO, PERFUM-
ING THE AIR AROUND YOU
WITH THE PROMISE OF
THE RICH BREW TO COME.

DESIGNERS
**JENNIFER
MORLA AND
SHARRIE
BROOKS**
SAN FRANCISCO
CALIFORNIA

TYPOGRAPHIC SOURCE
IN-HOUSE

STUDIO
MORLA DESIGN

CLIENT
**CHRONICLE
BOOKS**

PRINCIPAL TYPES
**ORATOR,
BODONI BOOK,
AND HELVETICA
BOLD**

DIMENSIONS
9 x 5½ IN.
(22.9 x 14 CM)

The similarity of espresso to other good-quality coffees starts and ends with the arabica coffee bean, because espresso means, first of all, a certain blend of coffee beans, a blend that depends on the coffee roaster's individual taste. Espresso also means a color of roasted beans, specifically a dark roast, though the degree of darkness also depends on the roaster's preference. After roasting, the beans are finely ground into an espresso grind, which may vary slightly depending on the kind of espresso machine being used. The espresso grind then must be brewed by the espresso method, which is different from other brewing methods in that it uses pressure to force water through the coffee grounds, rather than allowing gravity to draw water through the grounds. The drink that results from all these fine particulars is—if the espresso maker has followed all the right steps—the hot, black, lightly textured, fine-foam-covered, deeply flavored drink that we call espresso.

The first commercial espresso machines were manufactured in Italy in 1903, and the drink soon became the quintessential coffeehouse beverage. Today it has spread to other countries and is no longer an exclusively urban drink—espresso is found everywhere, in small towns and villages and even on some country roads, and in any kitchen with an espresso maker and a jar of dark-roast beans.

Almost all the taste of coffee comes from its aroma, and it's the aroma that reaches our senses first: wafting out of the kitchen when someone else is already up and has started the coffee, bursting out of the brown paper bag or canister when we open it to grind the day's first coffee beans, layering the air of city streets.

26. Mai bis 31. Juli 1994   Jüdisches Museum im Berlin Museum

Di bis So: 10 bis 20 Uhr

Martin–Gropius–Bau   Stresemannstraße 110

Traces of the Unborn — Daniel Libeskind in Berlin

Bill Drenttel
Stephen Doyle

DESIGNER
UWE LOESCH
DÜSSELDORF GERMANY

TYPOGRAPHIC SOURCE
IN-HOUSE

CLIENT
**JÜDISCHES
MUSEUM IN
BERLIN MUSEUM**

PRINCIPAL TYPE
**DIN
ENGSCHRIFT**

DIMENSIONS
$46^{7}/_{8}$ x $66^{1}/_{8}$ IN.
(119 x 168 CM)

DESIGNER
STEPHEN DOYLE
NEW YORK NEW YORK

TYPOGRAPHIC SOURCE
IN-HOUSE

STUDIO
**DRENTTEL
DOYLE
PARTNERS**

CLIENT
**AMERICAN
CENTER FOR
DESIGN**

PRINCIPAL TYPE
NEWS GOTHIC

DIMENSIONS
22 x **17** IN.
(55.9 x 43.2 CM)

Patrons Night

6:00 7:00 331 94 00:9

$

DESIGNER
**BENJAMIN
BAILEY**
NEW YORK NEW YORK

TYPOGRAPHIC SOURCE
IN-HOUSE

STUDIO
**THE ABELSON
COMPANY**

CLIENT
**MALLARY
MARKS**

PRINCIPAL TYPES
**NICHOLAS
COCHIN
(REDRAWN) AND
ENGRAVER'S
GOTHIC**

DIMENSIONS
$8^1/2$ X 11 IN.
(21.6 X 27.9 CM)

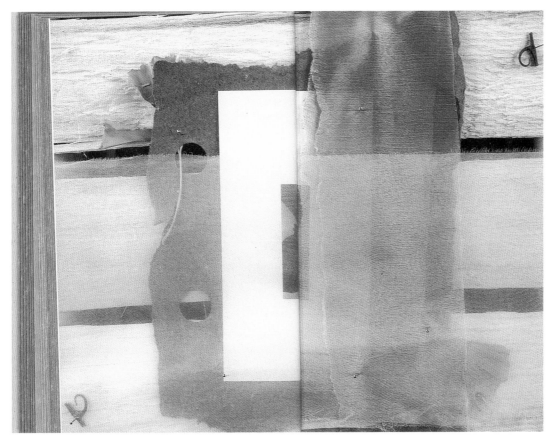

DESIGNER
TAKAAKI
MATSUMOTO
NEW YORK NEW YORK
TYPOGRAPHIC SOURCE
IN-HOUSE
STUDIO
MATSUMOTO
INCORPORATED
CLIENT
THE GALLERY
AT
TAKASHIMAYA
PRINCIPAL TYPES
BEMBO AND
COURIER
DIMENSIONS
5³/₄ x 8 IN.
(14.6 x 20.3 CM)

Cloth. So much a part of our everyday lives, it is easily taken for granted. Indeed, the manufacture of textiles constitutes one of the oldest continuous industries known to human beings, dating back at least 35,000 years to when our ancestors first began shaping animal skins and hair to produce garments. It took another 25,000 years until the discovery that twisting fibers together created strands which in turn could be interwoven to form fabrics. From this breakthrough, experimentation with fibrous materials such as cotton from plants and wool from animals has yielded a plethora of textile possibilities. The basic concept and its realization—textiles and the identification of raw materials from the environment that were capable of being spun and woven—"represented a major leap forward in thinking about the world and how it can be made more amenable to human life."[1] Furthering the quest for practicality, scientific discoveries in the nineteenth and twentieth centuries have revolutionized the textile industry by increasing the range of possible materials to include those that have been chemically reconfigured and synthetically fabricated.

Cloth provides the connecting thread linking the five artists—Han Feng, Ava Gerber, Jim Hodges, Beverly Semmes, and John Swanger—included in "Material Dreams." All employ diverse media but, in one way or another, incorporate fabric in their artworks to evoke a dreamlike, ethereal ambience. Not unlike alchemists or magicians, they transform

humble materials from everyday life into otherworldly, haunting artworks. All delight in the malleability of fabric—in shaping, draping, stretching, folding.

This fascination with cloth is hardly new; the fluidity of fabric has long captivated artists. Throughout the history of art, the depiction of drapery has been employed to simultaneously reveal and conceal the human form. Painters and sculptors were judged by their ability to render the softness of satin or the coarseness of wool in paint or marble. Shimmering pleats and cavernous folds offered fertile terrain for the play of light and shadow, conveyed by feathery brushstrokes or the solid three-dimensionality of cast bronze. Over the centuries, a rich vocabulary of geometric, near-abstract forms has been established to depict cloth, nearly constituting a genre in and of itself. For example, in seventeenth-century Italian painting and sculpture, drapery became a means for conveying spiritual and emotional content through a play of abstract forms; at times, it seemed to take on a life of its own.[2]

Often the material of choice for the artists in "Material Dreams" is one that reveals its woven origins, that is, fabric so light and so translucent that its warp and weft are clearly visible. The fabrics employed provide points of departure for extended reveries, for they are nearly as insubstantial and ephemeral as dreams themselves. Taking a cue from the Surrealists, who determined that the unconscious, trances, and

[14]

[15]

DESIGNER
GERALDINE
HESSLER
NEW YORK NEW YORK

ART DIRECTOR
FRED
WOODWARD

TYPOGRAPHIC SOURCE
IN-HOUSE

STUDIO
ROLLING STONE

CLIENT
ROLLING STONE

PRINCIPAL TYPE
SMOOKLER

DIMENSIONS
12 x 20 IN.
(30.5 x 50.8 CM)

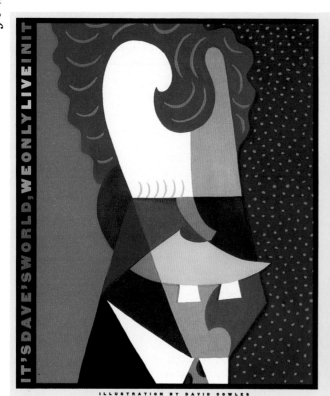

IT'SDAVE'SWORLD,WEONLYLIVEINIT

ILLUSTRATION BY DAVID COWLES

BY FRED SCHRUERS

MAN OF THE YEAR

DAVID LETTERMAN

ON A FRIDAY NIGHT IN MANHATTAN, not quite an hour after putting *Late Show* episode No. 211 in the can, David Letterman broods aloud over how the show went. His post-mortem, spilling out in a windowless conference room 12 floors above the Ed Sullivan Theater while taxi horns bray down on Broadway, is a characteristically disgruntled one. "Yeah," he says, "I wasn't very pleased with any aspect of the show. The audience and I never got together. And for me, that's a lost cause. If you can't win those people over,

ROLLING STONE, DECEMBER 29, 1994-JANUARY 12, 1995 · 31

DESIGNER
GEORGE
ESTRADA
SEATTLE WASHINGTON
LETTERER
GEORGE
ESTRADA
TYPOGRAPHIC SOURCE
IN-HOUSE
STUDIO
MODERN DOG
CLIENT
K2
SNOWBOARDS

DESIGNER
TODD
WATERBURY
PORTLAND OREGON

TYPOGRAPHIC SOURCE
PERSONAL
COLLECTION

AGENCY
WIEDEN &
KENNEDY

CLIENT
THE COCA-COLA
COMPANY

PRINCIPAL TYPE
MODERN
CONDENSED
GOTHIC

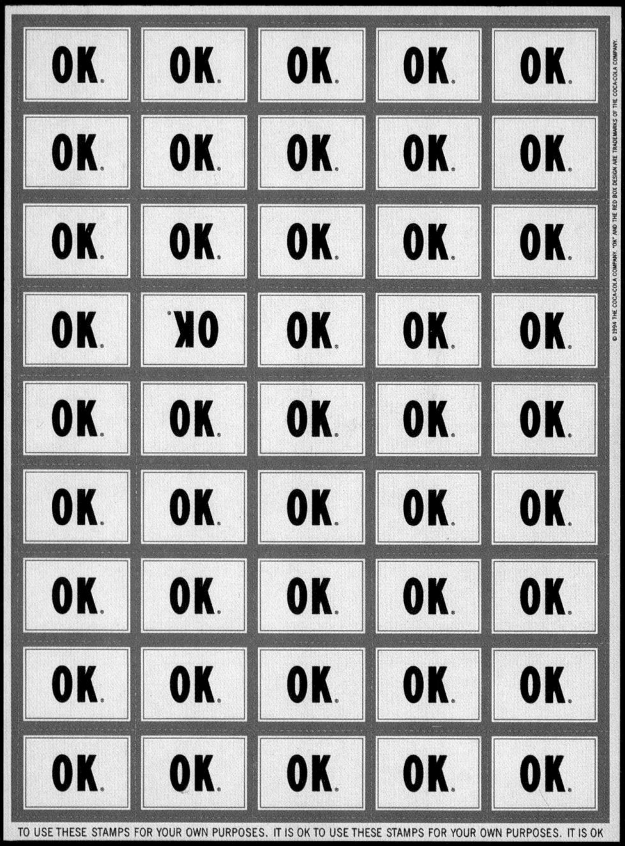

DESIGNER
CURT
SCHREIBER
CHICAGO ILLINOIS

DESIGN DIRECTOR
DANA ARNETT

TYPOGRAPHIC SOURCE
IN-HOUSE

STUDIO
VSA PARTNERS,
INC.

CLIENT
CHICAGO BOARD
OF TRADE

PRINCIPAL TYPES
FUTURA AND
AKZIDENZ
GROTESK

DIMENSIONS
11 X 14 IN.
(27.9 X 35.6 CM)

"Sell it at **4"** **4"**
"Sell it at
4"

As the world's leading futures exchange, the CBOT is continually challenged to maintain its leadership position and often finds itself the target of speculation among its competitors and newspaper headlines around the globe. In 1992, the CBOT proved all skeptics wrong and once again reaffirmed its position as the unsurpassed industry leader.

The CBOT's new volume record, an impressive achievement in itself, signifies the important role the exchange plays in the world's risk management strategies. Further, it is a direct tribute to the ongoing confidence placed in the exchange markets by its customers worldwide.

Through the hard work and dedication of the exchange membership, and staff, the CBOT has consistently provided a diverse base of deep, liquid markets on which the world's investors have come to rely. During the past year, the exchange continued in that tradition as both its financial and agricultural contracts expanded to unprecedented levels.

Volume in the CBOT's financial complex, which includes the CBOT's bellwether 30 Year U.S. Treasury bond futures contract—the most actively traded financial vehicle in the world, increased nearly 14 percent above 1992 levels. While T-bond futures led the way with a new annual trading record of 79,428,474, volume in the CBOT's Ten-, Five- and Two-Year U.S. Treasury note futures and options contracts soared to new heights as well. In fact, the CBOT Ten-Year U.S. T-note

futures and options were listed as two of the four fastest growing U.S. contracts in 1993 and the Ten-Year T-note futures was the only U.S. futures contract included among the top ten fastest growing futures contracts in the world.

Increasingly, the outstanding growth experienced in the CBOT's financial contracts during the past several years has created new demands for additional space to accommodate those markets. The 1993 record order flow, brought that need to a climax.

In an effort to reduce some of the overcrowding, the exchange initiated and will soon complete a multi-million dollar renovation of the financial floor. As a result of this plan, which includes design improvements such as the construction of larger trading pits for the growing interest-rate complex and additional booth space, the exchange has already been able to generate more trading activity and more business. However, this is a short-term answer at best. Space continues to be one of the main obstacles challenging the continued growth and success of the CBOT. Space concerns are a paramount issue for the exchange Board of Directors who are committed to developing a solution that will meet the needs of the CBOT membership. On January 19, 1994 the CBOT membership approved, by a large margin, the purchase of the 327 S. LaSalle Street building which will be razed to accommodate a new state-of-the-art trading facility.

The record growth experienced in 1993 was not limited to financial

78 73 05

In 1993 the Chicago Board of Trade, the world's leading futures exchange, once again provided the important cry on which the world has come to rely—its renowned open outcry auction markets, that is. In doing so, the CBOT traded a worldwide record volume of 178,773,105 contracts—firmly establishing itself as the unparalleled leader in the international futures and options industry.

buy buy

sell sell

buy

sell

sell

buy

sell

buy sell

buy sell

DESIGNERS
**STEVEN
TOLLESON AND
JEAN ORLEBEKE**
SAN FRANCISCO
CALIFORNIA

TYPOGRAPHIC SOURCE
IN-HOUSE

STUDIO
**TOLLESON
DESIGN**

CLIENT
**ASYST
TECHNOLOGIES,
INC.**

PRINCIPAL TYPE
GARAMOND

DIMENSIONS
7³/₄ x 5¹/₄ IN.
(19.7 x 13.3 CM)

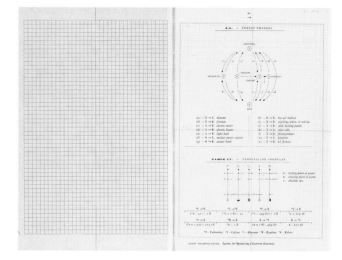

DESIGNER
DESIGN!
DALTON GEORGIA

TYPOGRAPHIC SOURCE
IN-HOUSE

STUDIO
DESIGN!

CLIENT
INTERFACE
FLOORING
SYSTEMS

PRINCIPAL TYPE
SABON

DIMENSIONS
9 X 12 IN.
(22.9 X 30.5 CM)

A cultural revolution is taking place at Interface. An integrated system of human and social values is emerging. A new way of thinking. A new way of working. A new way of doing business for employees and customers alike. Educating. Empowering. Transferring environmental issues from marketing to production. Responding with commitment. Leading with a new **direction.**

DESIGNER
HELFRIED
HAGENBERG
DÜSSELDORF GERMANY

TYPOGRAPHIC SOURCE
JÖSCHLI
DÜSSELDORF

STUDIO
HELFRIED
HAGENBERG

CLIENT
FACHBEREICH
DESIGN,
FACHHOCHSCHULE
DÜSSELDORF

PRINCIPAL TYPES
FRUTIGER AND
FUTURA

DIMENSIONS
33¹/₁₆ X 23³/₈ IN.
(84 X 59.4 CM)

FH D
FB 2

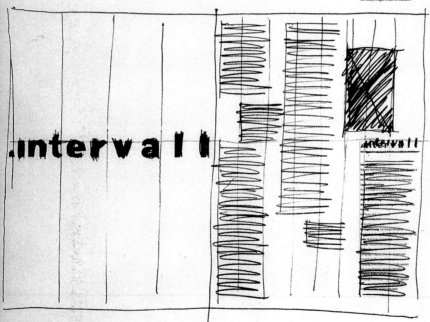

.intervall
Der Orientierungspunkt steht am Anfang,
das Ende ist offen.
Gestalterische Konstanten werden variabel,
die Variabilität zur Konstanten
Die Leitlinie für Inhalt und Layout liegt in
der Mitte und dient der Horizonterweiterung.
.intervall
Ein neues Magazin, das nie erscheint.

Uwe Loesch über die virtuelle
Realität eines erfolgreichen Flops:
.intervall
Donnerstag, 3. Februar 1994
14 Uhr, Raum N 1.40
Fachbereich Design
Fachhochschule Düsseldorf
Eine Veranstaltung zum Thema
Supplementdesign.

BY JEFF GOODELL

"A network is what I've always wanted in life"

Barry Diller The Rolling Stone Interview

DESIGNERS
FRED
WOODWARD
AND GAIL
ANDERSON
NEW YORK NEW YORK

ART DIRECTOR
FRED
WOODWARD

TYPOGRAPHIC SOURCE
IN-HOUSE

STUDIO
ROLLING STONE

CLIENT
ROLLING STONE

PRINCIPAL TYPES
ROMAN
COMPRESSED
AND BUREAU
GROTESQUE

DIMENSIONS
12 x 20 IN.
(30.5 x 50.8 CM)

DESIGNER
JOHN SAYLES
DES MOINES IOWA

LETTERER
JOHN SAYLES

TYPOGRAPHIC SOURCE
IN-HOUSE

STUDIO
SAYLES
GRAPHIC
DESIGN

CLIENT
PLANNED
PARENTHOOD OF
GREATER IOWA

PRINCIPAL TYPE
HANDLETTERING

DIMENSIONS
9⁷/₁₆ x 12⁷/₁₆ IN.
(24 x 31.6 CM)

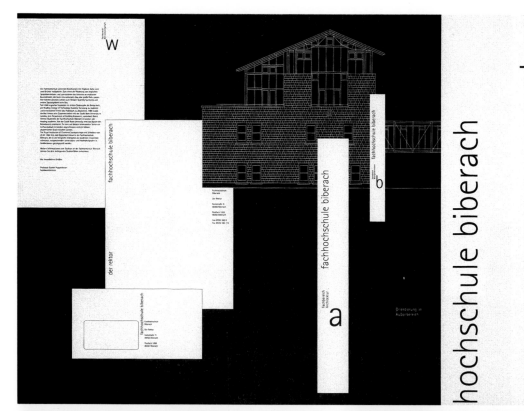

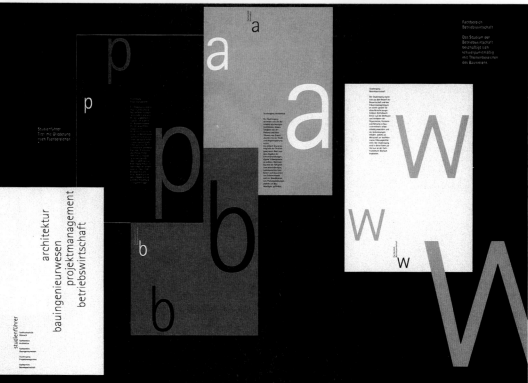

DESIGNER
GERD BAUMANN
SCHWÄBISCH GMÜND
GERMANY

CALLIGRAPHER
GERD BAUMANN

TYPOGRAPHIC SOURCE
IN-HOUSE

STUDIO
BAUMANN &
BAUMANN, BÜRO
FÜR
GESTALTUNG

CLIENT
ACADEMY OF
ARCHITECTURE,
BIBERACH

PRINCIPAL TYPES
ROTIS SERIF 55
AND ROTIS
SERIF 65

DIMENSIONS
8¼ x 11¹¹⁄₁₆ IN.
(21 x 29.7 CM)

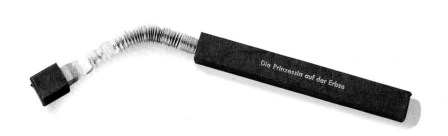

DESIGNER
ANDRÉ
MAASSEN
WUPPERTAL GERMANY

TYPOGRAPHIC SOURCES
IN-HOUSE AND
DRUCKEREI B.
REHRMANN
GMBH

STUDIO
ATELIER FÜR
KOMMUNIKA-
TIONSDESIGN
MAASSEN/
FRANKE

CLIENT
DRUCKEREI B.
REHRMANN
GMBH

PRINCIPAL TYPE
FUTURA

DIMENSIONS
118⅝ X 4½ IN.
(300 X 11.5 CM)

DESIGNER
CHRIS FROETER
CHICAGO ILLINOIS

TYPOGRAPHIC SOURCE
IN-HOUSE

AGENCY
VSA PARTNERS, INC.

CLIENT
CHICAGO
VOLUNTEER LEGAL
SERVICES
FOUNDATION

PRINCIPAL TYPE
CLARENDON

DIMENSIONS
7½ X 9 IN.
(19.1 X 22.9 CM)

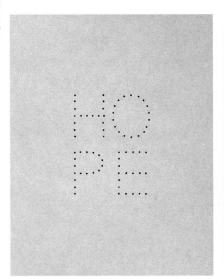

CVLS, born in an era of boundless optimism, marks this 30th Anniversary Year at a time of deepening public skepticism. We are bombarded with too much information about injustices too removed from our control. The temptation is to close our eyes and harden our hearts while waiting for others to devise a perfect systemic solution.

But people can't wait for the "cure." Too many clients need help now. One lawyer can't abolish homelessness, but he can fight a retaliatory eviction and keep one person off the streets. One lawyer can't eradicate poverty, but she can stop an unlawful garnishment from impoverishing one family. Last year 11,243 clients received some measure of justice, thanks to the efforts of 1,700 CVLS volunteers.

CVLS volunteers steadfastly and stubbornly improve the law one case, one client at a time. They represent the indomitable spirit of mankind.

Our impressive wall of plaques holds no inscription more eloquent than what this client wrote about her CVLS lawyer: "I think he is one of the kindest and calmest attorneys. He made me feel secure. He made me feel less poor. I feel really confident with him. Listen, we are very lucky to have such good volunteer service."

Jerome L. Nowaczewski
President of the Board

M. Lee Witte
Executive Director

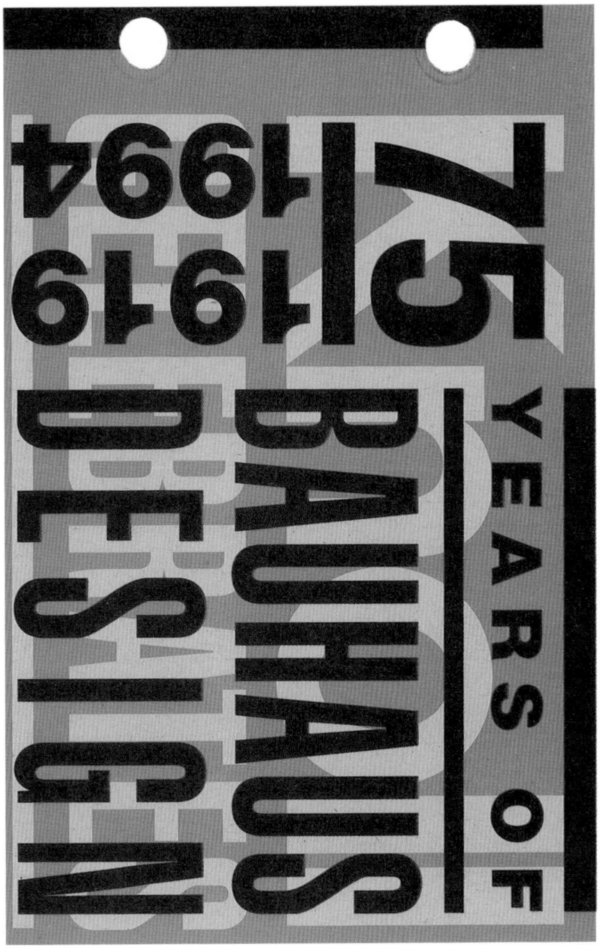

think

JOHN RIZZI • Interaction Tables, 1991

DESIGNER
CHRIS SOLWAR
NEW YORK NEW YORK

TYPOGRAPHIC SOURCE
IN-HOUSE

STUDIO
KNOLL
GRAPHICS

CLIENT
THE KNOLL
GROUP

PRINCIPAL TYPE
ADOBE NEUE
HELVETICA

DIMENSIONS
VARIOUS

77

DESIGNER
BILL DAWSON
HOLLYWOOD
CALIFORNIA

TYPOGRAPHIC SOURCE
IN-HOUSE

STUDIO
**TWO HEADED
MONSTER**

CLIENT
**WCCO-TV
CHANNEL 4,
MINNEAPOLIS**

PRINCIPAL TYPE
**FRANKLIN
GOTHIC HEAVY**

A-Büro **Orange**

A-Büro **Orange**

Liebe Freundin, lieber Freund,

DESIGNER
MONIKA IRMER
DÜSSELDORF GERMANY

ART DIRECTOR
KLAUS HESSE

TYPOGRAPHIC SOURCE
IN-HOUSE

STUDIO
HESSE
DESIGNAGENTUR
GMBH

CLIENT
ARCHITECTS
HEGER, SCHAD

PRINCIPAL TYPE
ITC OFFICINA

Hofaue 59
D-42103 Wuppertal   A-Büro **Orange**

Student Standards for the
Readiness
Academy

The **Edison** Project

Student Standards for the Junior
Academy

The **Edison** Project

Standards for History, Geography,
Civics, Economics

IN HISTORY, STUDENTS WILL BE ABLE TO:

Standards for
History

Standards for
Geography

IN GEOGRAPHY, STUDENTS WILL BE ABLE TO:

DESIGNERS
MATS
HAKANSSON,
KATRIN SCHMITT-
TEGGE, AND
GARY TOOTH
NEW YORK NEW YORK

CREATIVE DIRECTORS
STEPHEN DOYLE
AND TOM
KLUEPFEL

TYPOGRAPHIC SOURCE
IN-HOUSE

STUDIO
DRENTTEL DOYLE
PARTNERS

CLIENT
THE EDISON
PROJECT

PRINCIPAL TYPES
NEWS GOTHIC
AND GARAMOND

DIMENSIONS
VARIOUS

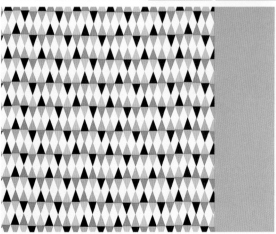

P

Primary
Student Standards for the
Academy

DESIGNERS
**BART CROSBY
AND ANGELA
NORWOOD**
CHICAGO ILLINOIS

TYPOGRAPHIC SOURCE
IN-HOUSE

STUDIO
**CROSBY
ASSOCIATES, INC.**

CLIENT
**CHAMPION
INTERNATIONAL
CORPORATION**

PRINCIPAL TYPE
**MONOTYPE
NEWS GOTHIC**

DIMENSIONS
**6 × 9 IN.
(15 × 22.9 CM)**

C

6

calcium carbonate

CaCO₃, a naturally occurring substance found in a variety of sources, including chalk, limestone, marble, oyster shells, and scale from boiled hard water. Used as a filler in the alkaline paper manufacturing process, calcium carbonate improves several important paper characteristics, like smoothness, brightness, opacity, and affinity for ink; it also reduces paper acidity. It is a key ingredient in today's paper coatings.
see also alkaline papermaking, ingredients of paper

Sources of calcium carbonate

calendering

the process of finishing a sheet of dried paper by pressing it between the highly polished metal cylinders of a calender "stack." The calender smoothes the paper by compression.
see also finish, papermaking, smoothness, supercalendering

An early calender

caliper

the thickness of a single sheet of paper, as measured with a sensitive tool called a micrometer, and expressed in units of thousandths of an inch. Caliper is a critical measure of uniformity. Excessive variation in caliper can lead to print variation, undesirable visual effects, and uneven stretch or press-feeding problems. It can also create problems in folding and binding.
see also bulk, thickness

A modern calender in use
**"Calender" comes to us
from the Latin
"cylindrus," for cylinder
or roll.**

case binding

see binding

cast-coating

paper produced with a surface that is a reasonably accurate replication of some other surface. To manufacture cast-coated paper, a paper web with wet or moistened coating is brought into contact with a polished chrome drum surface, which is replicated in the coated sheet.

There are two basic cast-coating technologies: the "wet process," invented and developed by Champion in 1937; and the "re-wet" process. Both methods remain in use to produce the world's output of cast-coated products. The advantage of the "wet process," used to manufacture Champion Kromekote, is that the sheet is both smooth and absorbent, not just smooth, allowing for excellent ink transfer with minimal pressure. Cast coated papers allow inks to set and dry quickly, making wet trapping easier and minimizing dot gain.

In general, cast-coated papers uniquely combine a superior flat

A micrometer, for measuring the caliper of a sheet of paper

surface with excellent ink receptivity, making them the best of printing surfaces, regardless of the type of printing process.
see also coated paper, dot gain, finish, smoothness, wet trap

cellulose fiber

the main component of the walls of all plant cells, cellulose gives plants their structural support and makes plant material fibrous. Both cotton and wood fibers are mostly made up of cellulose.
see also fiber, ingredients of paper, paper, pulping wood

chemical pulping

manufacturing pulp by pressure-cooking wood or other raw fibrous material into its component parts with solutions of various chemical liquors. The predominant chemical pulping process is the sulfate (kraft) process.
see also kraft, papermaking, pulping wood

clay

a naturally occurring substance commonly used in the paper industry. Clay is used as both a filler and a coating ingredient. By adding clay, papermakers can improve a paper's smoothness, brightness, opacity, and affinity for ink.
see also additives, coated paper, filler, ingredients of paper, opacity

coated paper

paper with an outer layer of coating applied to one or both sides. The coating may be added while the paper is still moving through the papermaking machine, or after it comes off the machine.

Coated papers are available in a variety of finishes, like gloss, dull, and matte. They tend to have good ink holdout and minimal dot gain, which can be especially important for recreating sharp, bright printed images, black and white halftones, and four-color process images. The smooth surface of coated papers also helps to reflect light evenly.
see also cast-coating, clay, dot gain, dull coated, four-color process, gloss, halftone, ink holdout, matte coated, off-machine coating

Colorcurve™ System

a color matching system based on light reflectance curves rather than on ink formulations. It is intended to coordinate colors across a variety of surfaces and materials and to reduce metamerism.
see also match color, metamerism, PANTONE MATCHING SYSTEM™, Toyo™

C

7

**Kromekote Coated One
Side – Kromekote C1S –
has one of the smoothest
paper surfaces. It's coated on both sides, but one
of the sides has a mirror-like finish "cast" onto it,
using heat, pressure, and
a chromium-plated drum.**

**Cast-coating was introduced by Champion in
1937.**

Kaolin clay

**The demand for coated
paper stock exploded in
1930 with the publication
of *Life* magazine.**

Paper collars from the 1800s

**Over the past 1,800
years since its invention,
we've found many ways
to use paper – from
room screens and panels
in the eighteenth century, to collars and cuffs in
the nineteenth century,
to plates and cups today.**

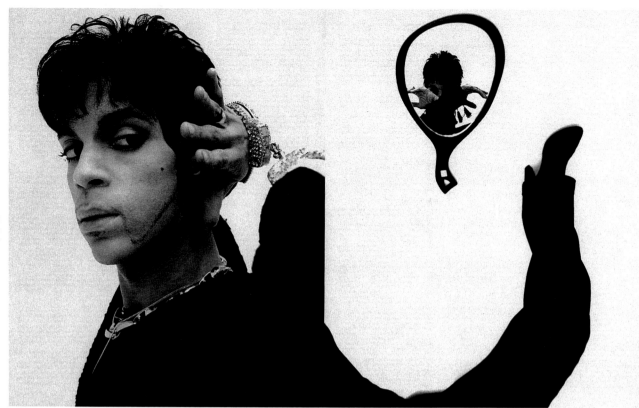

DESIGNER
DIDDO RAMM
NEW YORK NEW YORK

TYPOGRAPHIC SOURCE
IN-HOUSE

STUDIO
VIBE MAGAZINE

CLIENT
VIBE MAGAZINE

PRINCIPAL TYPES
PRN-GENEVA
AND BERTHOLD
GARAMOND

DIMENSIONS
12 X 20 IN.
(30.5 X 50.8 CM)

DESIGNER
ANDRÉ MAASSEN
WUPPERTAL GERMANY

TYPOGRAPHIC SOURCES
IN-HOUSE AND
DRUCKEREI B.
REHRMANN GMBH

STUDIO
ATELIER FÜR
KOMMUNIKATIONS-
DESIGN MAASSEN/
FRANKE

CLIENT
DRUCKEREI B.
REHRMANN GMBH

PRINCIPAL TYPE
FUTURA
CONDENSED

DIMENSIONS
7¹/₁₃ X 7¹/₄ IN.
(18 X 18.5 CM)

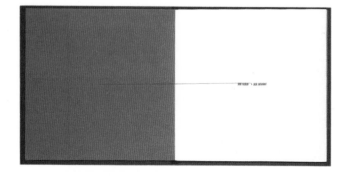

*The man
who won't be Prince
speaks at last about his
new name, his new attitude,
and a new body of work we may
never get to hear. After a yearlong
chase, Alan Light catches the
elusive superstar under a
cherry moon in Monaco.
Photographs by Dana
Lixenberg*

PROLOGUE
*Monte Carlo
May 2, 1994*

"SO HOW CAN WE DO AN INTERVIEW THAT'S
not like an interview?" asks ♀, as he spoons a dollop of jam into his tea. We're sitting in the Côté Jardin restaurant in Monte Carlo's historic Hôtel de Paris, overlooking a small garden that overlooks the Mediterranean Sea. He is here to accept an award for Outstanding Contribution to the Pop Industry at the 1994 World Music Awards. I am here at his request, the final step in a full year of putting together his

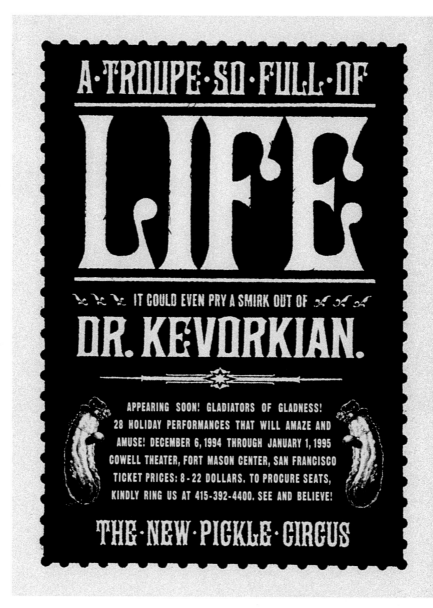

DESIGNER
MICHAEL
RYLANDER
SAN FRANCISCO
CALIFORNIA

LETTERER
DAN X. SOLO
OAKLAND CALIFORNIA

COPYWRITER
TOM WIT

TYPOGRAPHIC SOURCE
SOLOTYPE

AGENCY
THE IVORY
TOWER

CLIENT
THE NEW
PICKLE CIRCUS

PRINCIPAL TYPES
HYDE AND
MAIGRET

DIMENSIONS
6¹/₂ x 9 IN.
(16.5 x 22.9 CM)

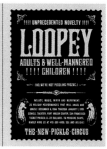

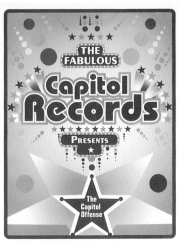

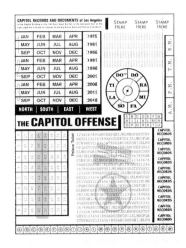

DESIGNERS
MICHAEL
STRASSBURGER,
ROBYNNE RAYE,
AND GEORGE
ESTRADA
SEATTLE WASHINGTON

LETTERERS
MICHAEL
STRASSBURGER,
ROBYNNE RAYE,
AND GEORGE
ESTRADA

TYPOGRAPHIC SOURCE
IN-HOUSE

STUDIO
MODERN DOG

CLIENT
CAPITOL
RECORDS,
LOS ANGELES

PRINCIPAL TYPES
AKZIDENZ
GROTESK,
BAUHAUS,
MADRONE,
AND HAND-
STENCILING

DIMENSIONS
8¹/₂ x 11 IN.
(21.6 x 27.9 CM)

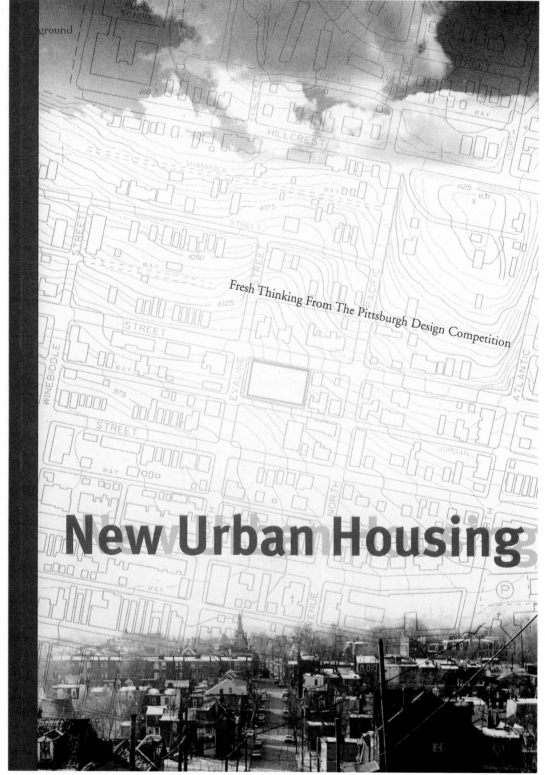

Fresh Thinking From The Pittsburgh Design Competition

New Urban Housing

DESIGNER
HUGO T. CHENG
PITTSBURGH
PENNSYLVANIA

TYPOGRAPHIC SOURCE
IN-HOUSE

STUDIO
MAYA DESIGN
GROUP, INC.

CLIENT
COMMUNITY
DESIGN CENTER
OF PITTSBURGH

PRINCIPAL TYPES
META AND
ADOBE
GARAMOND

DIMENSIONS
8¼ x 11½ IN.
(21 x 29.2 CM)

DESIGNER
MISSY WILSON
MINNEAPOLIS MINNESOTA

LETTERER
MISSY WILSON

TYPOGRAPHIC SOURCE
IN-HOUSE

STUDIO
DUFFY DESIGN

CLIENT
SMARTWOOL

PRINCIPAL TYPES
STYMIE, HIGHWAY
GOTHIC, AND
HANDLETTERING

61 9.4 81.0 6 0 9 f ax 41 8 3

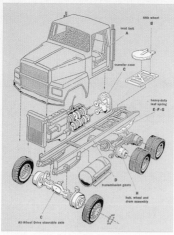

fifth wheel
B

seat belt
A

transfer case
C

heavy-duty
leaf spring
E-F-G

transmission gears
D

hub, wheel and
drum assembly

H

All-Wheel Drive steerable axle

Automotive Products Several member companies manufacture products for the transportation industry. Among them are (A) AM-SAFE, INC., (B) FONTAINE FIFTH WHEEL CO., (C) MARMON-HERRINGTON CO., (D) PERFECTION HY-TEST CO., (E) TRIANGLE AUTO SPRING CO., (F) CANADIAN SPRING OPER-ATIONS LTD., (G) DETROIT STEEL PRODUCTS CO., INC. and (H) WEBB WHEEL PRODUCTS, INC.

ECOWATER SYSTEMS, INC. **Water Conditioning** The world's largest manufacturer of residential water treatment systems, EcoWater Systems has manufactured water softeners since 1925. The reverse osmosis drinking water system (pictured here) fits conveniently under the sink and provides great-tasting, high-quality water.

JAMESWAY INCUBATOR COMPANY LTD. **Incubators and Hatchers** Jamesway manufactures incubators and hatching equipment for hatcheries around the world. Chicken, duck or turkey eggs are placed in an incubator for 18 days, then transferred to a hatcher for three days, where the animals emerge from their eggs. A Jamesway system can hold up to 105,000 eggs at one time.

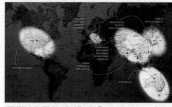

GETZ BROS. & CO., INC. **International Marketing** The nation's largest non-commodity export marketing and distribution company, Getz Bros. operates in more than 20 countries on four continents. The company markets agricultural products, biomedical products, industrial/technical products, consumer goods and commercial interiors through a variety of distribution channels.

THE MARMON GROUP

MANUFACTURING AND SERVICES

The Marmon Group is an international association of more than sixty autonomous member companies. The following portfolio represents a sample of the products and services offered.

1/2" X 60'

— VARIOUS DIAMETERS —

1/4"

3/4"

3"

5"

CERRO COPPER PRODUCTS CO. **Copper Tubing** With its sister company Cerro Copper Tube Co., Cerro Copper Products manufactures more copper tubing than any other company in the world. Each year, Cerro extrudes more than 200 million pounds of copper tubing for plumbing applications and for manufacturers of air conditioners, refrigerators and other products.

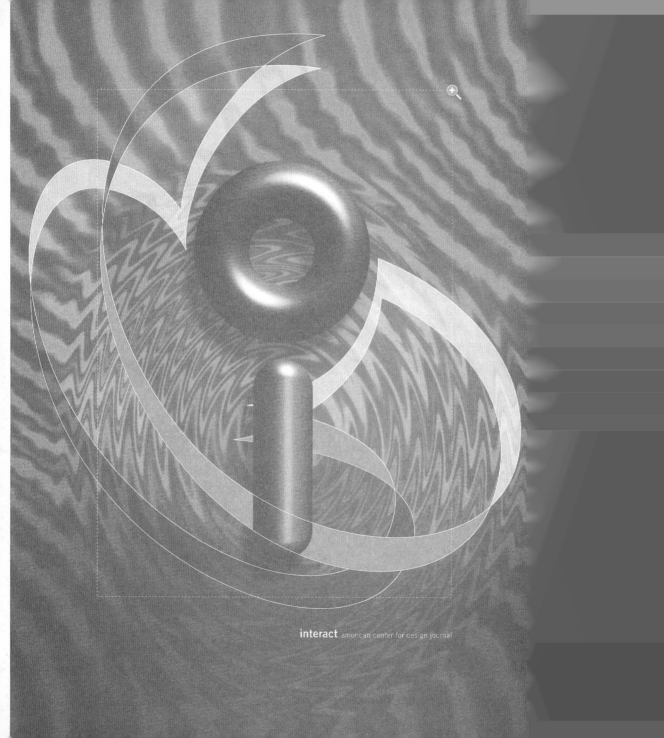

interact american center for design journal

Contents

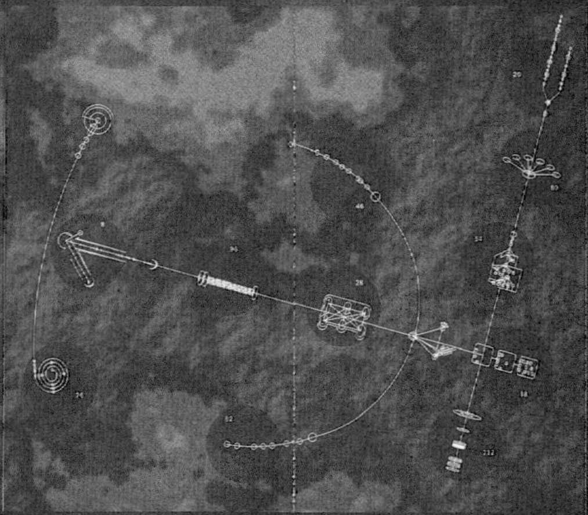

Additional icons refer to CD-ROM features not included in this printed journal.

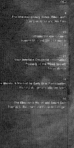

The Interdisciplinary Dance (Shall We?)

LAURRALEE ALBEN AND JIM FARIS

"WILL YOU, WON'T YOU, WILL YOU, WON'T YOU, WILL YOU JOIN THE DANCE?"

Lewis Carroll, Alice's Adventures in Wonderland, 1865

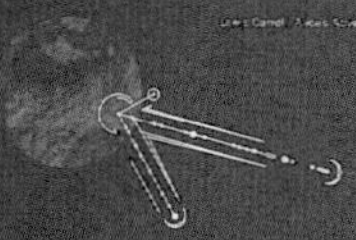

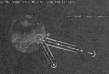

Author's note

[illegible]

Editor's note

[illegible]

Where there is an open mind, there will always be a frontier.

Charles Kettering

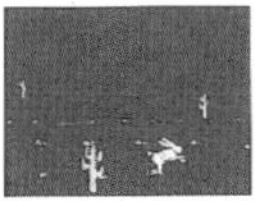

On with the dance! Let joy be unconfined; No sleep till morn, when Youth and Pleasure meet To chase the glowing Hours with flying feet.

Lord Byron, *Childe Harold's Pilgrimage*, 1812-18, canto 3, stanza 12

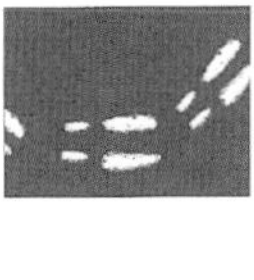

DANCING ON THE FRONTIERS

On the American frontier, settlers gathered together for corn husking frolics, quilting bees and barn raisings. Once the work was done, they often turned to dancing. The human need for self-expression and collaboration is not bound by time or place. Today this need manifests itself in the new frontier of multimedia.

The creation of multimedia is an interdisciplinary dance. Depending on the scope of the project, development teams may include content experts, cognitive psychologists, graphic and interface designers, instructional designers, programmers, writers, animators, video and sound producers and "media wranglers." These experts dance in just as intricate and varied a way as any square dancers. The result in both cases is a product of how well the individuals have danced together.

The dances of the early pioneers reflected their concern with survival and daily activities like hunting for food. In the square dance called Chase a Rabbit, the caller beckons, "First couple out of the couple on the right. Chase a rabbit, chase a squirrel. Chase a pretty girl round the world..."

Dances made an important connection between pioneer families, friends and neighbors who often lived many miles apart from each other. "To spread the word of the upcoming event, a man might stand on the steps of the general store and shout, 'Junket! Junket!'," according to Richard Kraus. "When a crowd had gathered, he would give the details of the dance. The selected meeting place might be in the store itself, in a barn, or even in a farm house kitchen. When it was scheduled to be held in a kitchen, all the furniture would have to be cleared out - even the stove. Sometimes only the woodbox would be left for the fiddler to stand on, with plenty of room for his well rosined bow to scrape away."

In a similar spirit of informality, invention and creative improvisation, an industry grew from the garages of Silicon Valley. Like the American frontier, the technological frontier requires rapid adaptation to changing circumstances. Often it is necessary to abandon rigid concepts and

be(a)ware

TRENT REZNOR OF NINE INCH NAILS PREACHES THE DARK GOSPEL OF **SEX, PAIN AND ROCK & ROLL**

LOVE IT TO DEATH

BY JONATHAN GOLD

Tables sprout candles in the darkened control room as thick and as numerous as mushrooms on a dank forest floor, and miniskirted department-store mannequins are scattered about in various states of bon-

DESIGNER
**KRISTINE
MATTHEWS**
SEATTLE WASHINGTON

TYPOGRAPHIC SOURCE
IN-HOUSE

STUDIO
**THE TRAVER
COMPANY**

CLIENT
**SEATTLE
DESIGN CENTER**

PRINCIPAL TYPE
**BERNHARD
MODERN**

PHOTOGRAPH BY ANTON CORBIJN

DESIGNERS
**FRED
WOODWARD AND
GAIL ANDERSON**
NEW YORK NEW YORK

ART DIRECTOR
**FRED
WOODWARD**

TYPOGRAPHIC SOURCE
IN-HOUSE

STUDIO
ROLLING STONE

CLIENT
ROLLING STONE

PRINCIPAL TYPES
**BUREAU AGENCY
BOLD AND
GOUDY**

DIMENSIONS
**12 x 20 IN.
(30.5 x 50.8 CM)**

The ABCs of Enlightenment

Being an opening lecture for college freshmen (and their parents) on the fine art of getting a true education.

I've been teaching in colleges and universities off and on for about 25 years. That's 25 years of freshmen—students like yourselves, who soon will be eyeballing strange new roommates and discovering that clothes don't wash themselves. Most of us who are professors will devote our first class (your first class) this fall to the basics of the course: the killer reading list, the unforgiving deadlines for term papers, what miserable fate awaits you if you miss an exam. That kind of thing.

But I find myself recently tempted to put the lecture on course mechanics aside in favor of a more general talk on how to get a generous education—not just from professors and classes, but from the college at large, and for yourself in particular. If I do give that talk to my opening freshman class (and here I recall Oscar Wilde's remark that he could "resist everything except temptation"), it will be from this alphabet of notes.

Robert Day, Professor of English, Director of the O'Neill Literary House

ALPHABETS. In themselves they are interesting. So is college interesting in itself: as in learning for its own sake. You don't need to go to the Career Placement Office your first week on campus...

BASEBALL. Once when playing deep in the hole at shortstop, I thought of a metaphor that yoked baseball to life...

C. As in the grade: average. Avoid. You're not going to college to be average...

DELPHI. Go there. Between your sophomore and junior years...

EMULATION. I am thinking of E.M Forster...

FRENCH. Did you pick a college or university that does not require a foreign language?...

GAINSBOROUGH, THOMAS; Gershwin, Ira; Graham, Martha. (See Emulation.)

HOURS. Because you only attend classes about 15 hours a week...

I don't want to," she says. If you're a guy, you might think she means "maybe," and "maybe" means "yes." Even if you're right, you're wrong...

JEFFERSON, THOMAS. You probably think of him as the third president of the United States...

KNOW YOURSELF. (See Delphi.)

LESSING, DORIS; Lee, Robert E.; Lamb, Charles; Lear, Edward; Lucretius. (See Emulation.)

MURPHY. He was a campus dog of ours who was famous for begging hamburgers at student picnics...

NABOKOV, VLADIMIR. American novelist and literature professor who once had something like the following conversation with a student at Cornell University...

OXFORD ENGLISH DICTIONARY on Historical Principles Founded Mainly on the Materials Collected by the Philological Society...

PHONES. I was taught by a professor born in the 19th century. One of his professors had been taught by Henry Wadsworth Longfellow...

QUESTION. Of course. And often.

REED, JOHN; Rhys, Jean; Rousseau, Jean Jacques; Russell, Bill. (See Emulation.)

STRUNK AND WHITE. *The Elements of Style* by William Strunk, Jr., With Revision, an Introduction, and a Chapter on Writing by E.B. White. Third Edition. Macmillan Publishing Co., Inc. New York, London. $4.95.

THOMAS JEFFERSON. (See also JEFFERSON, THOMAS.)

VOLUNTARY. Somewhere I read a definition of a student as a person in zealous and voluntary pursuit of knowledge...

UNNECESSARY DRINKING. College and boozing are an old tradition. Bacchus was probably the president of a fraternity...

X-ING. "X is a letter, which, though found in Saxon words, begins no word in the English language." So writes Samuel Johnson in his 1755 *Dictionary of the English Language*...

WHY? Almost always a good question.

YOU. (See Zeal.)

ZEAL. Somewhere I read a definition of a student as a person in zealous and voluntary pursuit of knowledge...

WASHINGTON COLLEGE
in the State of MARYLAND

300 Washington Avenue
Chestertown, Maryland 21620-1197
410-778-7700 or 800-422-1782

DESIGNER
WINNIE HULME
ATLANTA GEORGIA

TYPOGRAPHIC SOURCE
FINE PRINT
TYPOGRAPHY

STUDIO
COMMUNICORP

CLIENT
WASHINGTON
COLLEGE

PRINCIPAL TYPE
ADOBE CASLON

DIMENSIONS
33 x 21 IN.
(83.8 x 53.3 CM)

DESIGNERS
STEVEN
TOLLESON
AND JENNIFER
STERLING
SAN FRANCISCO
CALIFORNIA

TYPOGRAPHIC SOURCE
IN-HOUSE

STUDIO
TOLLESON
DESIGN

CLIENT
BLACK BOOK
MARKETING
GROUP

PRINCIPAL TYPE
GARAMOND

DIMENSIONS
8³⁄₄ x 11¹⁄₂ IN.
(22.2 X 29.2 CM)

HANNE DARBOVEN Ihre Kunst gehört einer Zwischensphäre an, in der literarische und bildnerische Aspekte aufeinandertreffen. Sie arbeitet konzeptualistisch und äußerst systematisch. Zumeist bestehen ihre Arbeiten aus statistischen Tabellen, mathematischen Tafeln, formelhaften Aufzeichnungen. Die Zahlen selbst allerdings transportieren keine über sich selbst hinaus bedeutenden Inhalte. Sie sind konkret, zweckfrei und entfunktionalisiert, bringen aber Rhythmik und einen gewissen ornamentalen Rapport zum Ausdruck. Zum Teil hat sie ihr systematisches Vorgehen auch in Büchern zusammengefaßt. In anderen Arbeiten sind die Zahlen- und Leitsysteme mit Fotos und literarischen Zitaten kombiniert. Hanne Darbovens Arbeiten muß man gleichzeitig lesen und sehen.

Hanne Darbovens Installation Geigensolo besteht aus einem schwarzen Sockel, einer Miniaturgeige nebst Geigenkasten und einem innenliegenden Zettel (mit Signatur u. a.) sowie einem gerahmten Notenblatt. Die Grundausstattung des Kunstwerkes liefert die Künstlerin, der Käufer der Arbeit jedoch vollendet das Werk durch seine Aufstellung. Das Kunstwerk erhält in seiner Eigenschaft als Auflageobjekt und durch die Art und Weise seiner Aufstellung eine ganze Reihe von neuen Facetten. Die fiktive Präsentationssituation wird so zum Teil eines ästhetischen Konzeptes. Das Kunstwerk wird zum Ereignisobjekt, das die Frage nach den Gattungsgrenzen zwischen den Kunstbereichen neu stellt. Bleibt wird aber auch die Beziehung zwischen Künstler, Kunstwerk und Betrachter. Denn letzterer vollendet durch sein Inviroment das von der Künstlerin begonnene Werk.

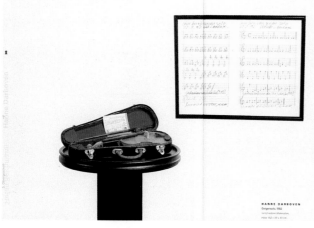

HANNE DARBOVEN
Geigensolo, 1992
Verschiedenen Materialien,
Höhe 102 × 33 × 33 cm

DESIGNER
KLAUS BIETZ
FRANKFURT GERMANY

TYPOGRAPHIC SOURCES
**IN-HOUSE
AND CON
COMPOSITION**

STUDIO
**HWL &
PARTNER DESIGN**

CLIENT
**MANNHEIMER
VERSICHERUNG AG**

PRINCIPAL TYPE
FRUTIGER

DIMENSIONS
**7⁷/₈ X 12³/₁₆ IN.
(20 X 31 CM)**

DESIGNER
BOB AUFULDISH
SAN ANSELMO
CALIFORNIA

STUDIO
**AUFULDISH
& WARINNER**

"bold"

saufy

more chunks

more fiber

Aa Bb Cc Dd Ee Ff Gg Hh Ii Jj Kk Ll Mm Nn Oo Pp Qq Rr Ss Tt Uu Vv Ww Xx Yy Zz

ABCDEFGHIJKLMNOPQRSTUVWXYZ

abcdefghijklmnopqrstuvwxyz

1!2@3#4$5%6^7&8*9(0)?

&c Hamburgefonstiv

DESIGNERS
CHARLES S. ANDERSON, TODD PIPER-HAUSWIRTH, PAUL HOWALT, AND JOEL TEMPLIN
MINNEAPOLIS MINNESOTA

ART DIRECTOR
CHARLES S. ANDERSON

TYPOGRAPHIC SOURCE
IN-HOUSE

STUDIO
CHARLES S. ANDERSON DESIGN COMPANY

CLIENT
CSA ARCHIVE

PRINCIPAL TYPES
20TH CENTURY AND FRANKLIN GOTHIC

DIMENSIONS
23 1/2 x 34 IN.
(59.7 x 86.4 CM)

KIRKI SCHULTZ

902 Grand Avenue, Suite 301, St. Paul, Minnesota 55105
Telephone (612) 293-9512 Pager (612) 350-8732

PHOTO STYLING/PRODUCTION

902 Grand Avenue, Suite 301, S.
Telephone (612) 293-9512 P.

KIRKI SCHULTZ

902 Grand Avenue, Suite 301, St. Paul, Minnesota 55105
Telephone (612) 293-9512 Pager (612) 350-8732

DESIGNER
DAVID
RICHARDSON
MINNEAPOLIS
MINNESOTA

TYPOGRAPHIC SOURCE
IN-HOUSE

STUDIO
KILTER
INCORPORATED

CLIENT
KIRKI SCHULTZ

PRINCIPAL TYPES
ORATOR AND
STAMP GOTHIC

DIMENSIONS
8½ x 11 IN.
(21.6 x 27.9 CM)

DESIGNERS
FRANCK
SARFATI, JOËL
VAN
AUDENHAEGE,
OLIVIER
STÉNUIT, AND
CHARLES VAN
HOORICK
BRUSSELS BELGIUM

LETTERERS
FRANCK
SARFATI, JOËL
VAN
AUDENHAEGE,
AND OLIVIER
STÉNUIT

TYPOGRAPHIC SOURCE
IN-HOUSE

STUDIO
|SIGN*|

CLIENTS
|SIGN*|,
AUNIPRINT, AND
CVH

PRINCIPAL TYPE
ATOMIZED
SQUARE 721
BOLD MEGA
EXTENDED
ULTRA ITALIC

DIMENSIONS
8¼ X 8¼ IN.
(21 X 21 CM)

DESIGNERS
SCOTT WADLER,
TIM MORSE,
AND TODD
BARTHELMAN
NEW YORK NEW YORK

TYPOGRAPHIC SOURCE
IN-HOUSE

AGENCY
MTV NETWORKS
CREATIVE
SERVICES

CLIENT
T.J. MARTELL

PRINCIPAL TYPE
TRADE GOTHIC
BOLD
CONDENSED #20

DIMENSIONS
VARIOUS

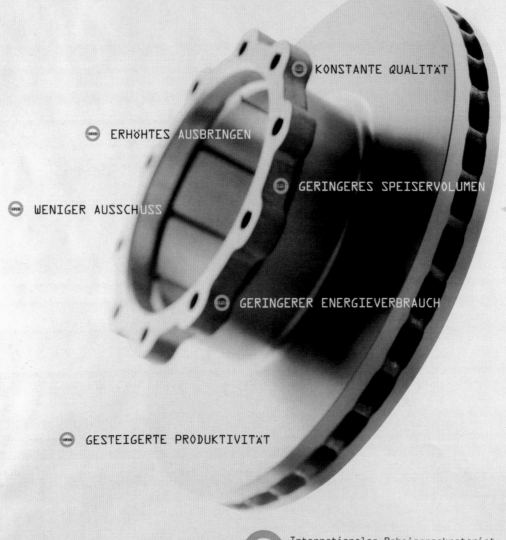

EIN · BRINGT MEHR · ROHEISEN ·

KONSTANTE QUALITÄT

ERHÖHTES AUSBRINGEN

GERINGERES SPEISERVOLUMEN

WENIGER AUSSCHUSS

GERINGERER ENERGIEVERBRAUCH

GESTEIGERTE PRODUKTIVITÄT

Internationales Roheisensekretariat
Breite Strasse 69, D-40213 Duesseldorf
Telefon: 0211.829.0

DESIGNERS
JAN KORNSTAEDT
AND NINJA
V. OERTZEN
DUISBURG GERMANY
TYPOGRAPHIC SOURCE
IN-HOUSE
CLIENT
INTERNATIONAL
PIG IRON
SECRETARIAT
(IPIS),
DÜSSELDORF
PRINCIPAL TYPE
OCR-A
DIMENSIONS
46¾ x 66⅛ IN.
(118.8 x 168 CM)

NucleusOne™

DESIGNER
JOSHUA DISTLER
BURLINGAME
CALIFORNIA

TYPOGRAPHIC SOURCE
IN-HOUSE

STUDIO
**JOSHUA DISTLER
DESIGN**

CLIENT
NUCLEUSONE

PRINCIPAL TYPE
NUCLEUSONE

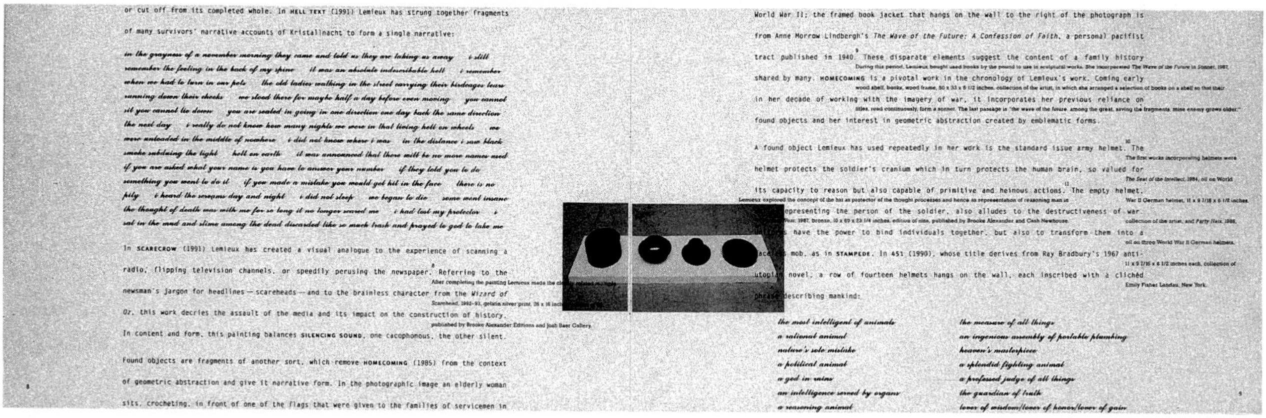

DESIGNER
ANITA MEYER
BOSTON MASSACHUSETTS

PHOTOGRAPHER
23

TYPOGRAPHIC SOURCE
MOVEABLE TYPE INC.

STUDIO
PLUS DESIGN INC.

CLIENT
DAVIS MUSEUM AND
CULTURAL CENTER

PRINCIPAL TYPES
COMMERCIAL SCRIPT,
LETTER GOTHIC,
META, AND ROCKWELL

DIMENSIONS
7³/₁₆ x 11⁵/₈ IN.
(18.2 x 29.5 CM)

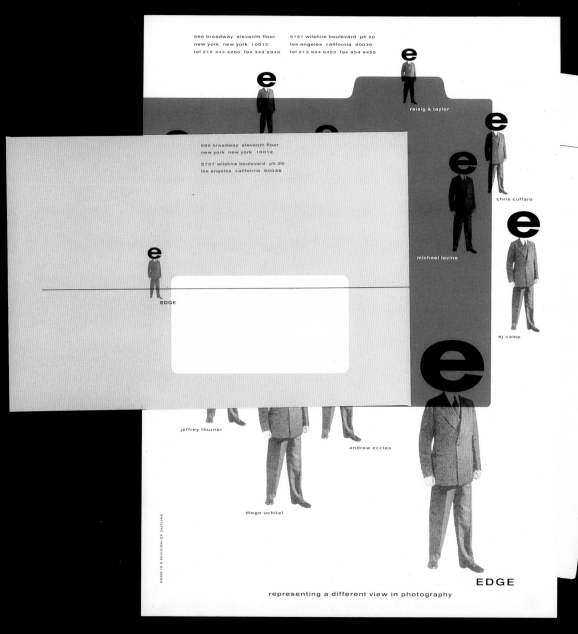

DESIGNER
TODD WATERBURY
PORTLAND OREGON

TYPOGRAPHIC SOURCE
IN-HOUSE

STUDIO
TODD WATERBURY

CLIENT
EDGE REPS

PRINCIPAL TYPE
**AKZIDENZ GROTESK
MEDIUM EXTENDED**

DIMENSIONS
VARIOUS

DESIGNER
**CURTIS
SCHREIBER**
CHICAGO ILLINOIS

TYPOGRAPHIC SOURCE
IN-HOUSE

STUDIO
**VSA PARTNERS,
INC.**

CLIENT
**MEAD FINE
PAPERS**

PRINCIPAL TYPE
FUTURA

DESIGN DIRECTOR
DANA ARNETT

DIMENSIONS
**2⅜ × 3⅜ IN.
(6 × 8.6 CM)**

DESIGNERS
**KOBE AND
ALAN LEUSINK**
MINNEAPOLIS MINNESOTA

LETTERERS
**KOBE AND
ALAN LEUSINK**

TYPOGRAPHIC SOURCE
IN-HOUSE

STUDIO
DUFFY DESIGN

CLIENT
**NATIONAL
COUNCIL ON
EDUCATION FOR
THE CERAMIC
ARTS (NCECA)**

PRINCIPAL TYPES
**STYMIE,
FRANKLIN, BELL
GOTHIC, TRADE
GOTHIC, AND
HIGHWAY GOTHIC**

DIMENSIONS
**18 × 35½ IN.
(45.7 × 90.2 CM)**

POSTER

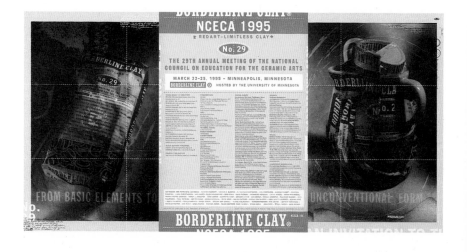

DESIGNER
BOB AUFULDISH
SAN ANSELMO
CALIFORNIA

TYPOGRAPHIC SOURCE
IN·HOUSE

STUDIO
**AUFULDISH
AND WARINNER**

CLIENT
EMIGRÉ

PRINCIPAL TYPES
**ZEITGUYS,
TRIPLEX, AND
MATRIX SCRIPT**

ZEITGUYS DESIGNERS
**ERIC DONELAN
AND BOB
AUFULDISH**
WHEATON ILLINOIS

SOUND DESIGNERS
**SCOTT PICKERING
AND BOB
AUFULDISH**
CLEVELAND OHIO

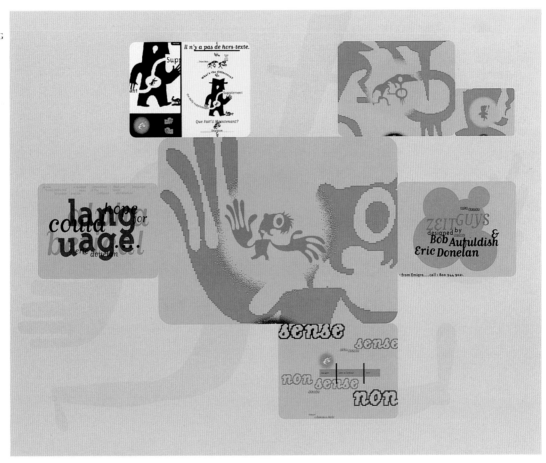

DESIGNER
JAMES MCKIBBEN
NEW YORK NEW YORK

TYPOGRAPHIC SOURCE
IN-HOUSE

CLIENT
CRANE & CO.

DESIGN DIRECTOR
**STEFF
GEISSBÜHLER**

PRINCIPAL TYPES
**ROTIS
AND UNIVERS**

DIMENSIONS
**7 × 9½ IN.
(17.8 × 24.1 CM)**

CRANE'S GLOBAL GUIDE

DESIGNER
CURTIS
SCHREIBER
CHICAGO ILLINOIS

DESIGN DIRECTOR
DANA ARNETT

TYPOGRAPHIC SOURCE
TRIBUNE SHOW
PRINT

STUDIO
VSA PARTNERS,
INC.

CLIENT
HARLEY-
DAVIDSON, INC.

PRINCIPAL TYPE
WOODBLOCKS

DIMENSIONS
20¹/₂ x 33 IN.
(52.1 x 83.8 CM)

POSTER

EAGLETHON

SUNDAY, SEPT. 11 - 1994

11:00 A. M. - 5:00 P. M.

CAPITOL DRIVE ENGINE & TRANSMISSION PLANT

11700 WEST CAPITOL DRIVE

Activities include: entertainment, music, children's area, fashion show, plant tours, H-D memorabilia auction, new motorcycle displays, motorcycle raffle.

●

ADMISSION $5.00
Includes commemorative Eaglethon Pin and motorcycle raffle ticket

●

ALL PROCEEDS TO MDA

THIS POSTER WAS MADE POSSIBLE THROUGH THE GENEROUS DONATIONS FROM THE FOLLOWING HARLEY-DAVIDSON "SUPPLIER/PARTNERS"
DESIGN: VSA PARTNERS, INC. PRINTING: HM GRAPHICS, INC. PAPER: CHAMPION CARNIVAL® SMOOTH TEXT, SOFT WHITE/70LB.

DESIGNERS
STEVE QUINN,
GREG SAMATA,
AND BRIAN
EHLERS
DUNDEE ILLINOIS

TYPOGRAPHIC SOURCE
IN-HOUSE

AGENCY
SAMATA
ASSOCIATES

CLIENT
SAMATA
ASSOCIATES FOR
SIMPSON PAPER
COMPANY

PRINCIPAL TYPE
FUTURA

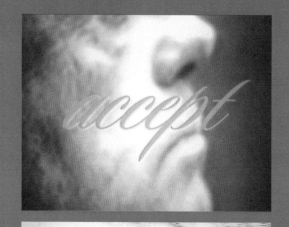

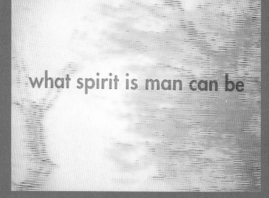

DESIGNER
LIONEL
FERVEIRA
ATLANTA GEORGIA

CREATIVE DIRECTOR
BOB WAGES

PHOTOGRAPHER
KEVIN IRBY
SAN FRANCISCO
CALIFORNIA

TYPOGRAPHIC SOURCE
IN-HOUSE

AGENCY
AXCESS GROUP

STUDIO
WAGES DESIGN

CLIENT
SHAW CONTRACT
GROUP, DIVISION
OF SHAW
INDUSTRIES,
INC.

PRINCIPAL TYPE
ITC GALLIARD
ROMAN

DIMENSIONS
20 X 32 IN.
(50.8 X 81.3 CM)

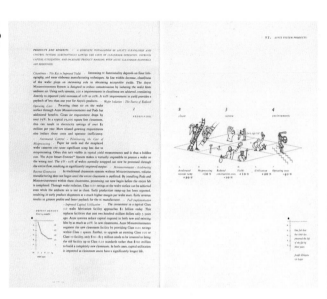

DESIGNERS
**STEVEN
TOLLESON AND
JEAN ORLEBEKE**
SAN FRANCISCO
CALIFORNIA

TYPOGRAPHIC SOURCE
IN-HOUSE

STUDIO
TOLLESON DESIGN

CLIENT
**ASYST
TECHNOLOGIES,
INC.**

PRINCIPAL TYPE
GARAMOND

DIMENSIONS
**6³⁄₄ x 10¹⁄₄ in.
(17.1 x 26 cm)**

DESIGNERS
DAVID J. HWANG,
BILL DAWSON,
AND
CHRISTOPHER
WARGIN
HOLLYWOOD
CALIFORNIA

TYPOGRAPHIC SOURCE
IN-HOUSE

AGENCY
BBDO/ BRASIL

STUDIO
TWO HEADED
MONSTER

CLIENT
PEPSI/BRASIL

PRINCIPAL TYPE
HELVETICA

DESIGNER
RÜDIGER GÖTZ
HAMBURG GERMANY

LETTERER
RÜDIGER GÖTZ

TYPOGRAPHIC SOURCE
IN-HOUSE

STUDIO
FACTOR DESIGN

CLIENT
WEST FUN
& FANTASY

PRINCIPAL TYPES
AKZIDENZ
GROTESK,
ALTERNATE
GOTHIC, AND
HANDLETTERING

DIMENSIONS
VARIOUS

DESIGNER
JO DAVISON
STRAND
MINNEAPOLIS
MINNESOTA

TYPOGRAPHIC SOURCE
IN-HOUSE

STUDIO
THE EDISON
GROUP

CLIENT
THE MINNESOTA
ORCHESTRAL
ASSOCIATION

PRINCIPAL TYPE
HELVETICA
CONDENSED

DIMENSIONS
5 1/2 x 8 1/2 IN.
(14 x 21.6 CM)

INVITATION

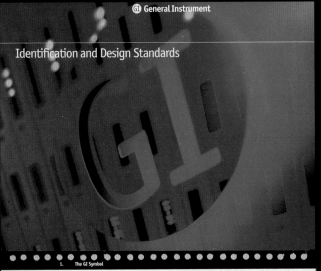

GI General Instrument

Identification and Design Standards

1.   The GI Symbol

The symbol is the unique visual styling of the initials "GI." It is one of the most important graphic elements used to identify the company and must be used on all materials coming from the corporation and the business units.

The symbol is based on the ITC Officina Sans typeface that is used throughout the program, however the individual letterforms of both the "G" and the "I" have been modified.

The GI within the circle should always be considered "transparent" so that the background on which the symbol is reproduced will always show through the GI.

All reproductions of the symbol must be made from original art available in either the Reproducible Materials section of this manual or from an official GI computer diskette. The symbol should never be redrawn, respaced or altered in any way except when special permission is granted by the Corporate Communications Department.

Symbols in the Reproducible Materials section are supplied by typographic point sizes and should be clipped directly from these printed sheets when needed for reproduction artwork.

When an extremely large size of the symbol is needed for signs, vehicles or exhibits, always enlarge the symbol from the 200 point masters found in the Reproducible Materials section.

The symbol may be reproduced in GI Green, black, gray or silver. It may be reversed to white out of any solid color, illustration or photograph so long as it remains recognizable. It may also be die cut out of, or etched or engraved into a variety of natural materials.

9.7   Literature and Advertising   Ring Binders   Various Formats

The standard binder format shown on the previous pages is for convenience and ease of preparation and should not stifle the creativity needed in designing covers for promotional materials or other information produced by the corporation. Illustrated below are covers which vary from the standard format but effectively present information within the identity program's guidelines.

DESIGNER
BART CROSBY
CHICAGO ILLINOIS

TYPOGRAPHIC SOURCE
IN-HOUSE

STUDIO
CROSBY
ASSOCIATES,
INC.

CLIENT
GENERAL
INSTRUMENT
CORPORATION

PRINCIPAL TYPE
ITC OFFICINA
SANS

DIMENSIONS
12¼ x 14 IN.
(32.4 x 35.6 CM)

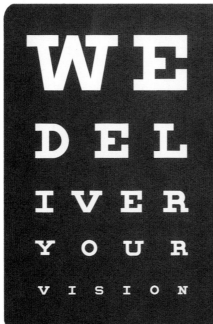

DESIGNER
JAMES KOVAL
CHICAGO ILLINOIS
LETTERER
GRANT DAVIS
TYPOGRAPHIC SOURCE
IN-HOUSE
DESIGN FIRM
**VSA PARTNERS,
INC.**
CLIENT
**MIDWEST
LITHO ARTS**
PRINCIPAL TYPE
MEMPHIS
DIMENSIONS
**7 x 10¼ IN.
(17.8 x 26 CM)**

understand

understanding is the essence of every vision. at midwest litho
arts. we remain committed to delivering the quality standards
you expect. our experienced representatives are trained to
listen and ask the right questions. we help you clarify your
objectives and interpret your goals for every assignment.

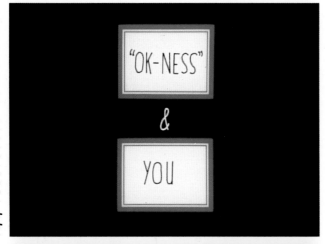

DESIGNER
TODD
WATERBURY
PORTLAND OREGON

WRITER
PETER WEGNER

DIRECTOR
PITTMAN
HENSLEY

TYPOGRAPHIC SOURCE
PITTMAN
HENSLEY

AGENCY
WIEDEN &
KENNEDY

CLIENT
THE COCA-COLA
COMPANY

PRINCIPAL TYPES
COURIER AND
ALTERNATE
GOTHIC

TELEVISION
COMMERCIAL

IS THERE ANY QUICK WAY TO MEASURE MY CURRENT LEVEL OF "OK-NESS"?

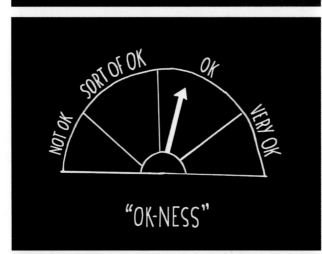

DESIGNER
TODD
WATERBURY
PORTLAND OREGON

LETTERER
TODD
WATERBURY

WRITER
PETER WEGNER

DIRECTOR
PITTMAN
HENSLEY

TYPOGRAPHIC SOURCE
IN-HOUSE

AGENCY
WIEDEN &
KENNEDY

CLIENT
THE COCA-COLA
COMPANY

PRINCIPAL TYPE
HANDLETTERING

DESIGNER
DIDDO RAMM
NEW YORK NEW YORK
TYPOGRAPHIC SOURCE
IN-HOUSE
STUDIO
VIBE MAGAZINE
CLIENT
VIBE MAGAZINE
PRINCIPAL TYPES
VIBRATION
GOTHIC AND
GARAMOND NO. 3
ITALIC
DIMENSIONS
12 × 20 IN.
(30.5 × 50.8 CM)

OF PHREAKS AND HACKERS

A brief sojourn among the young sultans of software and captains of code before the info highway paves this underground over.
By Carol Cooper. Illustrations by John Hersey

VIBE 77

DESIGNER
FOCUS 2
DALLAS TEXAS

TYPOGRAPHIC SOURCE
IN-HOUSE

STUDIO
FOCUS 2

CLIENT
DALLAS SOCIETY
OF VISUAL
COMMUNICATIONS

PRINCIPAL TYPE
CAUSTIC
BIOMORPH

DIMENSIONS
24 x 36 IN.
(61 x 91.6 CM)

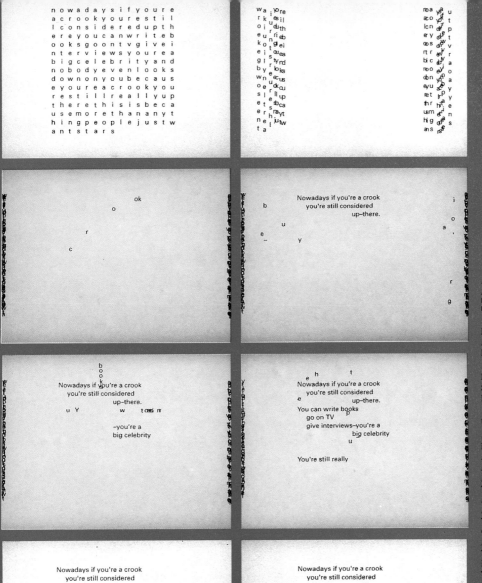

DESIGNER
AMY ROGACZ
PROVIDENCE RHODE
ISLAND

INSTRUCTORS
**DAVID PETERS
AND RONNIE
PETERS**

SCHOOL
**RHODE ISLAND
SCHOOL OF
DESIGN**

PRINCIPAL TYPE
UNIVERS 55

PROJECT
**DISASSEMBLE
A QUOTATION BY
ANDY WARHOL
AND ARRANGE
THE LETTERS IN
A SQUARE GRID.
ANIMATE THE
TYPE INTO A
COMPOSITION,
APPLYING THE
TRADITIONAL
RULES OF
TYPOGRAPHY:
CHARACTER AND
WORD SPACING,
LINE BREAKS,
CAPITALIZATION,
PUNCUATION, ETC**

DESIGNERS
PIA BETTON,
ANKE MARTINI,
BRIGITTE
HARTWIG,
RICHARD BUHL,
HARALD WELT,
AND CHRISTIAN
VOM KAMPTZ
BERLIN GERMANY

CALLIGRAPHER
ERIK
SPIEKERMANN

TYPOGRAPHIC SOURCE
CITY SATZ

STUDIO
META DESIGN

CLIENT
VERLAG HERMANN
SCHMIDT MAINZ

PRINCIPAL TYPE
WALBAUM
STANDARD BQ9

DIMENSIONS
4 13/16 x 7 3/16 IN.
(12.3 x 18.3 CM)

The well served portion: there's space for milk in this cup, just as normal letterspacing allows for uneven printing or ink squash.

The over-generous host: one stir produces a storm in a coffee cup, and an unhappy guest. Printing gravure, or on rough paper, requires more space between characters.

This cup runneth over: a full portion in an espresso cup is like reducing tight headline setting to eight point.

always to set WORDS IN CAPITALS one or two units wider than normal – it makes them easier to read and prevents them sticking out from the rest of the text like a sore thumb. In addition, one can set them half a size smaller than text size. Once the right calculations have been made and written into the typesetting program, you don't need to re-specify every time; unless, of course, you want to revise your decisions. In these days of miniaturisation type sizes are, after all, not restricted to whole units, or to any particular kind of unit: one can set in millimetres (and fractions) or points (either kind, and fractions) or inches; and, wonder of wonders, one can define type size in relation to capital height (it makes sense to measure something that's visible, doesn't it?).

The next hint may sound terribly banal to many people, but all the same there is a good reason for its appearance here. Almost every day I notice that people who order type – typographers, layout artists, production assistants – seem to forget to tell the compositor the final size at which the type will appear. (Here, in passing, a message to those who believe in ghosts and work in 'body' sizes: the aforesaid and hereafter-said only applies to headline setting, and to text matter to be displayed in giant sizes – on exhibition panels, for instance.) The consequence is that everything is set so tightly that only bricklayers could admire it! Lovely for sharp-edged headlines printed litho, but not so good for sub-headings in text, and bad for gravure and letterpress printing. Small sizes appear optically closer anyway, even without the image

51

DESIGNERS
YOO MI LEE
NEW YORK NEW YORK

CALLIGRAPHERS
ANDREAS
COMBÜCHEN AND
YOO MI LEE

CREATIVE DIRECTOR
ANDREAS
COMBÜCHEN

TYPOGRAPHIC SOURCE
IN-HOUSE

AGENCY
FRANKFURT
BALKIND
PARTNERS

CLIENT
FRANKFURT
BALKIND
PARTNERS

PRINCIPAL TYPES
BERNHARD,
HELVETICA, AND
NEWS GOTHIC
(MANIPULATED)

DESIGNERS
PAULA SCHER,
RON LOUIE, AND
LISA MAZUR
NEW YORK NEW YORK

TYPOGRAPHIC SOURCE
IN-HOUSE

STUDIO
PENTAGRAM
DESIGN

CLIENT
THE PUBLIC
THEATER

PRINCIPAL TYPES
MORGAN GOTHIC,
PAULAWOOD,
SERIWOOD, E TEN,
E SEVENTEEN,
E TWENTY-FIVE,
WOOD BLOCK
CONDENSED,
AND ALTERNATE
GOTHIC NO. 2

DIMENSIONS
VARIOUS

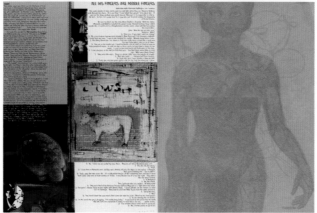

DESIGNER
SCOTT CLUM
SILVERTON OREGON

TYPOGRAPHIC SOURCE
IN-HOUSE

STUDIO
RIDE

CLIENT
BLUR MAGAZINE

PRINCIPAL TYPES
CYBEREROTICA
AND META

DIMENSIONS
8 x 10⅜ IN.
(20.3 x 27 CM)

DESIGNER
MYRON
POLENBERG
NEW YORK NEW YORK

LETTERER
GERARD HUERTA
SOUTHPORT
CONNECTICUT

PHOTOGRAPHER
JOHN MANNO

AGENCY
POLENBERG, INC.

STUDIO
GERARD HUERTA
DESIGN, INC.

CLIENT
SWISS ARMY
BRANDS

PRINCIPAL TYPE
HANDLETTERING

DESIGNER
BRENDÁN
MURPHY
CINCINNATI OHIO

LETTERER
BRENDÁN
MURPHY

STUDIO
BRENDÁN
MURPHY

CLIENT
MATDAN
AMERICA
CORPORATION

PRINCIPAL TYPES
CLARENDON,
GILL SANS, AND
HANDLETTERING

DIMENSIONS
11 × 8½ IN.
(27.9 × 21.6 CM)

LOGOTYPE
AND
CATALOG

Portland Brewing is committed to the creation of world class beers. This fierce dedication will energize our Company vision to be a quality supplier and employer as we increase share of mind and market to become a leader in the craft beer industry.

Portland Brewing

annual report · fiscal year 1994

Letter to our Shareholders, Employees, Customers and Friends: I am extremely delighted to write of our many successes during the last fiscal year ended June 30, 1994 (FY 94) and the first quarter ended September 30, 1994 of FY 95. We enjoyed tremendous growth and, simultaneously, made great strides to position the company for continued growth and future profitability. Business Review: First and foremost, Portland Brewing sold more than 25,000 barrels of beer in FY 94, an increase of more than 120% over FY 93. Gross revenues for the year more than doubled to nearly $4.5 million. These dynamic trends continued during the first quarter of FY 1995 (July-September): we sold nearly 10,800 barrels, more than double last year; and the $2 million gross revenue for the quarter nearly matched the revenue total for all of FY 93! Importantly, we are experiencing balanced growth: our home market of Oregon, with the largest sales base, continues to grow at a faster pace than the specialty category as a whole, thus making PBC the largest micro in the state to gain market share three years running. In Washington, sales increases of 100-200% per month have vaulted us into the state's Top 10 (which includes contract brewers Boston Beer Company and Pete's Brewing); the new market of Colorado, introduced in May 1994, has now surpassed expectations; the huge market of California is rapidly developing and the other expansion states continue to show very strong growth trends. Our strong distributor network now numbers more than 100 in nine western states, and as capacity comes on line we will expand into the emerging Arizona and New Mexico markets. Stock Offering Review: The company's 5-state Regulation A direct public offering was successfully completed in June 1994. We'd like to offer a special "Thank You and Welcome" to our 2700 new shareholders who purchased more than 465,000 shares, raising nearly $2.8 million. These proceeds were instrumental to our successful growth and were used for a number of important purposes, including: ◦ New equipment and tankage that have increased annual capacity to 58,000 barrels ◦ A new filler and other upgrades to the bottling line ◦ Construction and start-up of our on-site restaurant, The BrewHouse Taproom & Grill which opened in August ◦ Development of an array of marketing materials for our primary and seasonal brands. The Portland Brewing family now numbers more than 3500 stockholders of record. We'd like to thank each and every one of you. Industry Changes: As many of you are aware, the Northwest, and in particular Portland, are the center of the micro brewing revolution. The major American brewers have also noticed and reacted. Anheuser-Busch, the brewer of Budweiser beer and the world's largest brewing company, is forming an alliance with Seattle-based Red Hook Brewing. Anheuser-Busch is the first to seek such an alliance with a microbrewery, but Miller Brewing Co. has also expressed an interest and has spent a good deal of time studying specialty breweries nationwide. At the same time, major breweries are introducing micro-type products, new microbreweries are opening and more contract brews are being marketed. In addition, other large non-beer beverage companies seem to be exploring the possibility of participating in the micro category. No doubt the landscape will continue to change at an ever-increasing pace. The next year for Portland Brewing: Our hope is that the future holds more of the past. The goal for the current fiscal year is another 100% increase in sales volume, and first quarter results put us right on track. In addition, our plans include these key initiatives: ◦ Additional capital expansion and brewery improvements ◦ Continued market expansion and development ◦ New product development and introduction ◦ Programs to further solidify and strengthen our all-important distributor network ◦ Expansion of the BrewHouse Taproom & Grill. I want to express my gratitude to all of you who have made this such a terrific year. I want to especially thank and welcome our new shareholders, employees and distributors for joining the Portland Brewing team. Let's continue the pace, work together and make fiscal year 1995 the best one yet! Best regards, Charles A. (Tony) Adams, Chairman & President of Portland Brewing Company

DESIGNER
SALLY HARTMAN
MORROW
PORTLAND OREGON

TYPOGRAPHIC SOURCE
IN-HOUSE

STUDIO
SANDSTROM
DESIGN, INC.

CLIENT
PORTLAND
BREWING

PRINCIPAL TYPES
AVENIR,
MATRIX ITALIC,
AND TRIXIE

DIMENSIONS
8¹/₂ x 11 IN.
(21.6 x 27.9 CM)

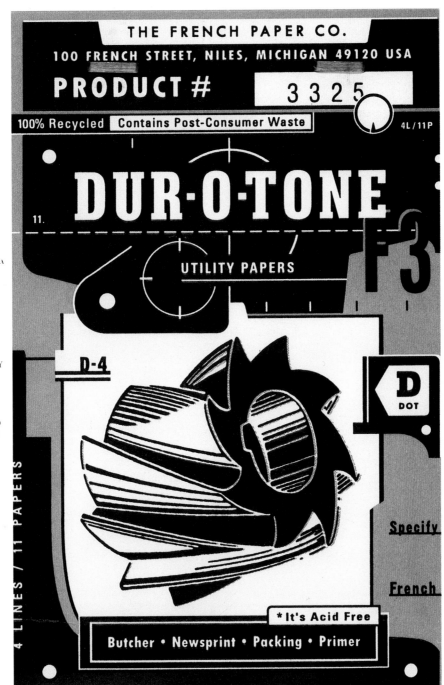

THE FRENCH PAPER CO.
100 FRENCH STREET, NILES, MICHIGAN 49120 USA
PRODUCT # 3325
4L/11P
100% Recycled · Contains Post-Consumer Waste

11.
DUR·O·TONE
F3
UTILITY PAPERS

D-4
D DOT

Specify

French

*It's Acid Free
Butcher · Newsprint · Packing · Primer

4 LINES / 11 PAPERS

DESIGNERS
CHARLES S.
ANDERSON AND
PAUL HOWALT
MINNEAPOLIS MINNESOTA
ART DIRECTOR
CHARLES S.
ANDERSON
TYPOGRAPHIC SOURCE
IN-HOUSE
STUDIO
CHARLES S.
ANDERSON
DESIGN COMPANY
CLIENT
FRENCH PAPER
COMPANY
PRINCIPAL TYPES
ROCKWELL BOLD
CONDENSED AND
20TH CENTURY
DIMENSIONS
4¼ x 6½ IN.
(10.8 x 16.5 CM)

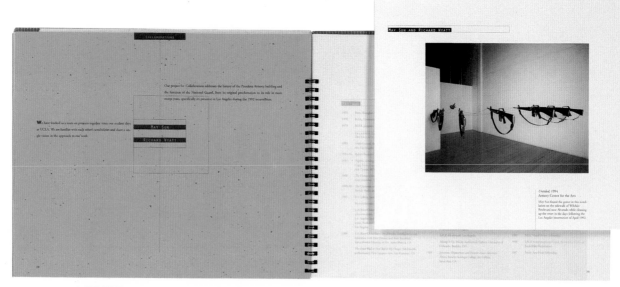

DESIGNERS
KIMBERLY BAER
AND MARGARET
VAN OPPEN
VENICE CALIFORNIA

STUDIO
KIMBERLY BAER
DESIGN
ASSOCIATES

CLIENT
PASADENA ART
ALLIANCE

PRINCIPAL TYPE
ADOBE
GARAMOND

DIMENSIONS
$9^{5}/_{8}$ X 12 IN.
(24.4 X 30.5 CM)

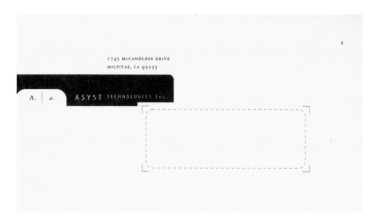

DESIGNERS
STEVEN
TOLLESON AND
JEAN ORLEBEKE
SAN FRANCISCO
CALIFORNIA

TYPOGRAPHIC SOURCE
IN-HOUSE

STUDIO
TOLLESON
DESIGN

CLIENT
ASYST
TECHNOLOGIES,
INC.

PRINCIPAL TYPES
ITC OFFICINA
AND HELVETICA
ROUNDED

DIMENSIONS
5$\frac{1}{2}$ x 3 IN.
(14 x 7.6 CM)

DESIGNER
MITCHELL MAUK
SAN FRANCISCO
CALIFORNIA

TYPOGRAPHIC SOURCE
IN-HOUSE

STUDIO
MAUK DESIGN

CLIENT
IN-FORM

PRINCIPAL TYPE
VARIOUS

DIMENSIONS
15 x 2$\frac{1}{2}$ x 2 IN.
(38.1 x 6.4 x 5.1 CM)
PACKAGING

DESIGNERS
ZEMPAKU SUZUKI
AND MASAHIRO
NAITO
SHINTOMI TOKYO JAPAN

LETTERER
YOICHI
HASHIKURA

ART DIRECTORS
JUN UENO AND
ZEMPAKU SUZUKI

ILLUSTRATOR
HANNA-BARBERA

COPYWRITER
MARIKO HAYASHI

TYPOGRAPHIC SOURCE
IN-HOUSE

AGENCY
DENTSU INC.

STUDIO
B•BI STUDIO INC.

CLIENT
THE TOYO TRUST
& BANKING CO.,
LTD.

PRINCIPAL TYPE
FRANKLIN GOTHIC

DIMENSIONS
28²/₃ x 40⁹/₁₆ IN.
(72.8 x 103 CM)

DESIGNER
PETRA
SOELTZER
DÜSSELDORF GERMANY

STUDIO
PROF. HELFRIED
HAGENBERG,
FACHBEREICH
DESIGN FH
DÜSSELDORF

CLIENT
FACHHOCHSCHULE
DÜSSELDORF

PRINCIPAL TYPE
ITC OFFICINA

DIMENSIONS
33¹/₁₆ x 23³/₈ IN.
(84 x 59.4 CM)

DESIGNER
SEAN ADAMS
LOS ANGELES
CALIFORNIA

TYPOGRAPHIC SOURCE
IN-HOUSE

STUDIO
ADAMS/MORIOKA

CLIENT
FILM FORUM

PRINCIPAL TYPES
BELL GOTHIC
AND TRADE
GOTHIC

DIMENSIONS
4 × 5 IN.
(20.3 × 12.7 CM)

Panelists including Erika Suderburg, David Ehrenstein and William Jones lead a discussion on contemporary media practices. What constitutes the "cutting-edge" and what are its agendas? How have these changed from historical antecedents? How do Hollywood and TV serve as sites for alternative media's cultivation, intervention, or commercial appropriation? Is the notion of a "cutting-edge" still viable today?

2.23.94
Wednesday
8:00 pm
Hollywood Moguls
FREE

Changing Channels: Media Arts in the '90s
Roundtable 1:
Questioning on / the "Cutting-Edge"
Co-presented with The Getty Center for the History of Art and the Humanities

Ni de aquí, ni de allá: Latinos/as in the Imagination of Southern California

Films and videos by Chicano/a media artists offering alternative visions to Hollywood's representation of the complex history of Latinos/as in the US. Set against D.W. Griffith's Ramona (1910) and featuring: David Avalos, Deborah Small, William Franco and Miki Seifert's Ramona: Birth of a mis-ce-ge-NATION (1992); Edgar Bravo's Mi Casa (1989); Sylvia Morales' Chicana (1979); Frances Salome Españás, El Espejo/The Mirror (1991); Sophie Rachmuhl's Marisela: Portrait of a Los Angeles Poet (1991); Harry Gamboa's Baby Kake (1985); Sandra Peña's Crónica de un Ser (1990); Melody Ramirez's Jezebel Spirit (1989); and Esperanza Vasquez's Agueda Martinez: Our People, Our Country (1977).

3.7.94
Monday
8:00 pm
Hollywood Moguls
Curated by
Christopher Ortiz

Nina Menkes' Magdalena Viraga: Story of a Red Sea Crossing

In Magdalena Viraga: Story of Red Sea Crossing (1986), Nina Menkes takes the viewer through the complex spiritual/political awakening of a benumbed prostitute accused of murder in downtown LA. The film's compelling intensity is drawn from the poetry of Gertrude Stein, Anne Sexton and Mary Daly, as well as from Tinka Menkes' enigmatic portrayal of the main character's emotional paralysis from abuse. This first feature was awarded Best Independent / Experimental Film by the Los Angeles Film Critics Association.

3.8.94
Tuesday
7:00 pm
Central Library
FREE

I'm an avid reader of your magazine, enjoying your articles immensely. But in "Quiet Storm," by Frank Owen [Dec. '93/Jan. '94], Andre Harrell is quoted as saying, "White critics always miss the art that's in the middle of the black community." That just shows the ignorance of the critics. That doesn't mean white people don't appreciate black R&B artists or their music—aside from the fact that there are white R&B artists, too. I am white, and definitely into hip hop, R&B, jazzamatazz, rap, etc. In fact, Babyface was right: rap introduced me to R&B. I began listening to the sounds of Public Enemy, Ice-T, Scarface, Dr. Dre, Tupac, and Ice Cube. I still do, but because of their sampling and use of R&B (e.g., Bobby Brown), I now listen to vintage New Edition, Boyz II Men, Jade, Shai, Toni Braxton, Tevin Campbell, and others. Wanting to make a career of my own vocal talents, I find myself trying to imitate K-Ci on Jodeci's rendition of "Lately." My point is: White people are down with the R&B culture, too. And sometimes we understand and even relate to the sounds of urban artists. Critics are critics, it's their job to be opinionated. But don't assume one race can't understand another race's music. Let me enjoy your articles as just a reader, not a "white reader." And to Andre Harrell and Frank Owen, let me be a listener, not a "white listener." AARON T. DRURY, CASPER, WY

I would like to take this opportunity to commend Mimi Valdes's "Those T.I.R.E.D. Acronyms" [Dec. '93/Jan. '94]. For a while, I was hoping that a writer would address this issue and let people know that these acronyms are now flavorless. As a big fan of R&B and hip hop, I gave INTRO their props when they first came out. I even thought the name had a little flavor going on. After reading the "T.I.R.E.D." piece, I said to myself, "That shit is wack." Innovative New Talent Reaching Out sounds like something their grandmother named them for their first talent show. On the other hand, imagine someone's grandmother naming their grandson's group Yaggfu Front. You can't tell me that these @&%#%@ don't experiment with homemade drugs. A nice homely word to describe this group is "corny." Yaggfu Front sounds like some incurable shit found under your toenail. And you know what's funny? They're probably home right now saying to themselves, "That shit is phat. How did we ever come up with such a name?" My guess is a defective game of Scrabble. O.F.T.B. should be sued by Off-Track Betting (O.T.B.). I'll bet you that one of them has a gambling problem. "T.I.R.E.D." was short, sweet, energetic, and to the point. It gets a 10 in my book. NAME WITHHELD, NEW YORK CITY

If I wanted to read an article on all the reasons why I should hate Jodeci, I would have gone to the jealous liars who spread stories about them, not bought this magazine. I hope DeVante uses his gun on you, Tom Sinclair, for calling him "lanky." If he was so hard to pin down, why didn't you put the spotlight on K-Ci, Jo-Jo, or Mr. Dalvin? ASHLEY WILLIAMS, ANNAPOLIS, MD

It amazes me to read these puff pieces on Jodeci ["Guns and Roses," Tom Sinclair, Dec. '93/Jan. '94] that fail to address the real reasons behind—and the tragedy of—their success. The two lead singers, the Hailey Brothers, were not strangers to the fame game. They recorded at least three albums on a gospel label—under the name of Little Cedric and the Hailey Singers. Sorry guys, but I just don't buy the "young boys who now have a little money and don't know how to adjust to fame" nonsense. These are young men who play a game with clearly defined parameters and who have chosen how to conduct their lives: young men who, in fact, have been playing since they were boys. The untold scandal, if there is one, is how they glorify themselves and turn their backs on what made them so good in the first place—namely, the Creator—who, if they were really in touch, would remind them of espousing humility, respecting a power greater than theirs, and self-respect, not self-aggrandizement. Oh yeah, and let's see, Jodeci, two million? Boyz II Men, seven million? Yo, DeVante, who's "going through the motions"? Better reach for that bow tie, brother. DONALD CLEVELAND, BROOKLYN, NY

Please understand that I considered myself an average, up-on-it, street-conscious, ruffneck, don't-give-a-shit, strictly-for-the-ladies kind of big dog. Then recently, I picked up an issue of Vibe and my day went from reality—"Hey, my man, what da hellsup? Check that. Yo, later-for-dem hoes; let's..."—to Dana Owens-land and {"It's Not Easy Being Queen," Lucy Kaylin, Dec. '93/Jan. '94}, where I saw the face of, and read the verbals communicated by, Ms. Owens. Then I imagined losing control; that in the presence of a woman like her, I'd become a virtual on-my-knees, baby-please, baby-baby here's some flowers and candy and anything you want, Dana, today, yes, this minute, sweetheart, kind of house-puppified mutt. Why, you ask? Because, Dana is both embodied beautifully and emotioned perfectly. And women like her are goddesses deserving of....Then I returned to reality, but slightly altered: "Who? Huh, hoes?!? Yo, dude, ain't no such thing." At least not among any sisters that I've seen. SAUL BROWN, SALT LAKE CITY, UT

We were dismayed to find the theme of "Gypsies and thieves" used to promote fashions in your magazine ["Kid: Who Are You," Hilton Als, Dec. '93/Jan. '94]. While all ethnic groups have their thieves, Gypsies included, Gypsies are not to be classified automatically with thieves, nor are the terms interchangeable. We are a nonwhite, ethnic minority of East Indian origin, numbering over one million in the country, have been recognized as such by the U.S. Bureau of the Census, and are protected as an ethnic minority under Title VII of the 1964 Civil Rights Act. Despite this, most Americans are not familiar with who or what we are, and remain ignorant of the facts that most Romani Americans came here after 1864, following the abolition of 550 years of slavery in the Balkans; and that we lost an estimated 75 percent of our total number in the Holocaust, and are enduring a sharp increase in racially motivated violence in Europe today. In 1992, *The New York Times* published the results of a public opinion poll that was conducted over a 25-year period and which included 58 ethnic and racial groups. During this period, Gypsies were at the bottom of the list as the most prejudiced-against minority in America. Since most Americans are not aware that we are here, these opinions must be based wholly upon media misrepresentation of our people. Magazines such as yours are the cause of this, and add to anti-Gypsy racism by reinforcing the notion that we are a race of thieves. SAM CONNICK, INTERNATIONAL ROMA FEDERATION, MANCHACA, TX

Editor's reply: "Kid: Who Are You?" did not equate Gypsies with thieves nor did it intend to degrade Gypsies. Gypses and Thieves is a clothing company whose clothes were featured in the story. If you take issue with their name, perhaps you should contact them.

DRIVEBY SHOOTING NEW YORK CITY GEOFFROY DE BOISMENU

VIBE 19

DESIGNERS
GARY KOEPKE
AND DIDDO
RAMM
NEW YORK NEW YORK

TYPOGRAPHIC SOURCE
IN-HOUSE

STUDIO
VIBE MAGAZINE

CLIENT
VIBE MAGAZINE

PRINCIPAL TYPES
GARAMOND
NO. 3, MEMPHIS,
HELVETICA 95,
AND
HELVETICA 55

DIMENSIONS
10 X 20 IN.
(25.4 X 50.8 CM)

Magic Board

DESIGNER
VITTORIO
COSTARELLA
SEATTLE WASHINGTON

LETTERER
VITTORIO
COSTARELLA

TYPOGRAPHIC SOURCE
IN-HOUSE

STUDIO
MODERN DOG

CLIENT
K₂ SNOWBOARDS

PRINCIPAL TYPE
CLARENDON
(MODIFIED)

DESIGNER
FRED
WOODWARD
NEW YORK NEW YORK

ART DIRECTOR
FRED
WOODWARD

TYPOGRAPHIC SOURCE
IN-HOUSE

STUDIO
ROLLING STONE

CLIENT
ROLLING STONE

PRINCIPAL TYPE
MONACO

DIMENSIONS
12 x 20 IN.
(30.5 x 50.8 CM)

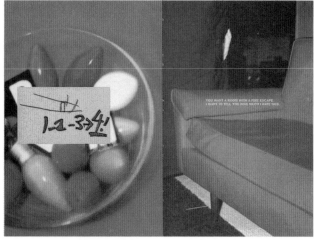

DESIGNERS
TOM RECCHION,
MICHAEL STIPE,
AND CHRIS
BILHEIMER
BURBANK CALIFORNIA
AND ATHENS GEORGIA

TYPOGRAPHIC SOURCE
IN-HOUSE

STUDIO
WARNER BROS.
RECORDS

CLIENT
WARNER BROS.
RECORDS

PRINCIPAL TYPE
HELVETICA
NEUE BLACK
ITALIC

DIMENSIONS
8¹/₂ x 6 IN.
(21.6 x 15¹/₄ CM)

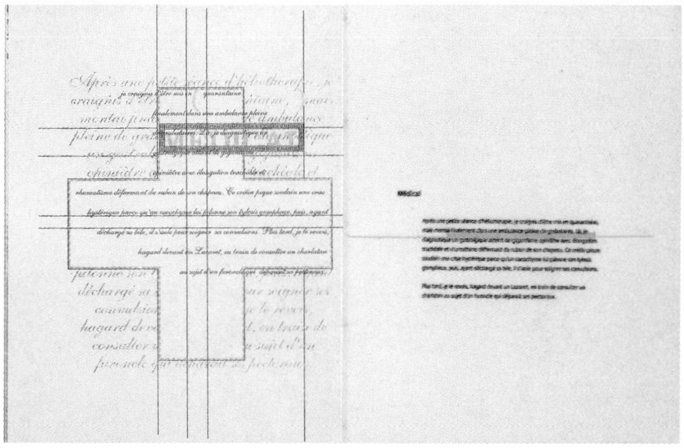

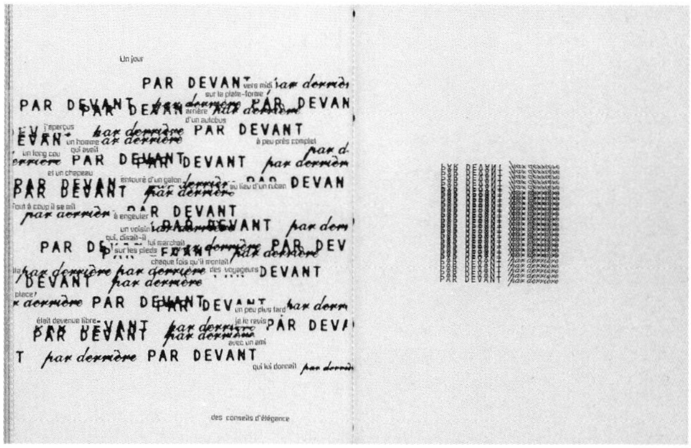

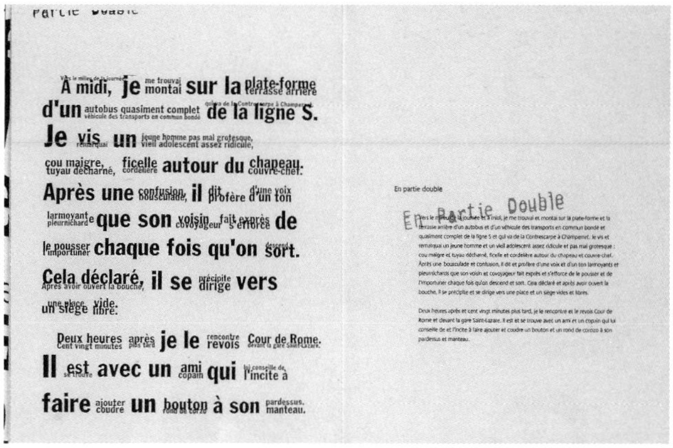

DESIGNER
JUDITH POIRIER
MONTREAL QUEBEC CANADA

ASSISTANT DESIGNERS
MAXINE FLORES,
DANIELLE
GINGRAS, AND
JUSTINE FOURNIER

TYPOGRAPHIC SOURCE
VARIOUS

AGENCY
DEPARTMENT
OF DESIGN,
UNIVERSITY
OF QUEBEC AT
MONTREAL (UQAM)

STUDIO
LES MAÎTRES
TYPOGRAPHES
ZIBRA

CLIENT
TYPOMONDO

PRINCIPAL TYPE
VARIOUS

DIMENSIONS
8 1/4 X 7 1/13 IN.
(21 X 18 CM)

SONGS *by* RICHARD THOMPSON

Beat the Retreat

featuring: R.E.M., DINOSAUR JR, DAVID BYRNE, BOB MOULD,
BONNIE RAITT, X, LOS LOBOS, SYD STRAW & EVAN DANDO,
SHAWN COLVIN & LOUDON WAINWRIGHT III,
GRAHAM PARKER, BEAUSOLEIL, THE FIVE BLIND BOYS OF ALABAMA,
JUNE TABOR, MADDY PRIOR & MARTIN CARTHY

DESIGNERS
CLIVE PIERCY
AND MICHAEL
HODGSON
SANTA MONICA
CALIFORNIA

TYPOGRAPHIC SOURCE
IN-HOUSE

STUDIO
PH.D

CLIENT
CAPITOL
RECORDS/TOMMY
STEELE

PRINCIPAL TYPES
GILL SANS,
BEMBO,
PERPETUA, AND
MATRIX SCRIPT

DIMENSIONS
5½ x 5 IN.
(14 x 12.7 CM)

DESIGNER
STEPHEN BANHAM
MELBOURNE AUSTRALIA

LETTERER
STEPHEN BANHAM

TYPOGRAPHIC SOURCE
IN-HOUSE

STUDIO
THE LETTERBOX

CLIENT
THE LETTERBOX

DIMENSIONS
3 x 4⅛ IN.
(7.4 x 10.5 CM)
BOOKLET

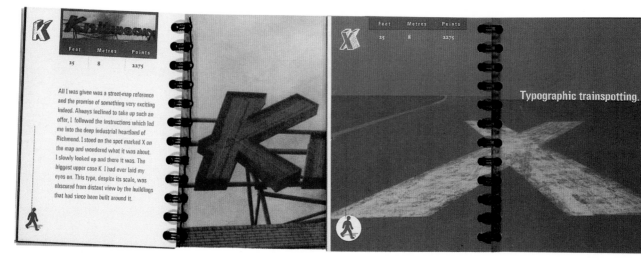

Alles
Listen /
Lists
everywhere

DESIGNER
KLAUS HESSE
DÜSSELDORF GERMANY

TYPOGRAPHIC SOURCE
IN-HOUSE

STUDIO
**HESSE
DESIGNAGENTUR
GMBH**

CLIENT
**FACHHOCHSCHULE
DORTMUND**

PRINCIPAL TYPE
SYNTAX

DIMENSIONS
$33^1/_{16} \times 23^5/_8$ IN.
(84 x 60 CM)

Alles Listen / Lists everywhere, **12. Focus Workshop Dortmund 1994**
Wettbewerb, Ausstellung, Diskussionen, Competition, Exhibition, Events, **Einsendeschluß,** Date of Entry **31.08.1994**
Museum für Kunst und Kulturgeschichte Dortmund, Fachhochschule Dortmund, Parsons School of Design New York

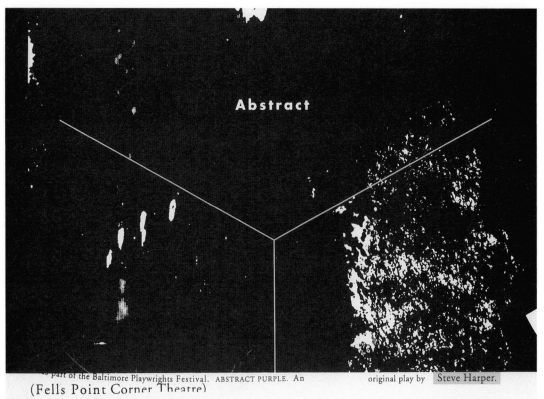

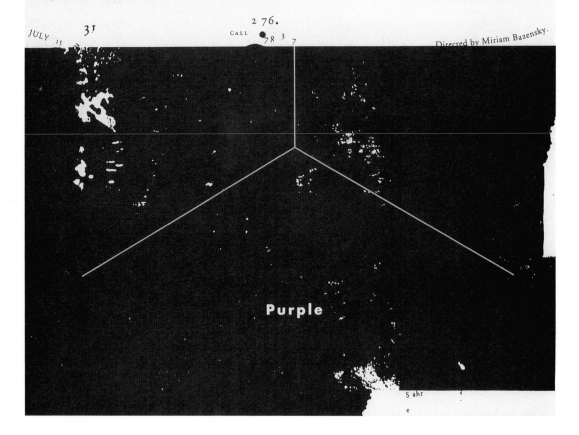

DESIGNER
PAUL SAHRE
BALTIMORE MARYLAND

TYPOGRAPHIC SOURCE
IN-HOUSE

CLIENT
FELLS POINT
CORNER
THEATRE

PRINCIPAL TYPES
FUTURA AND
ADOBE
GARAMOND

DIMENSIONS
13½ x 20 IN.
(34.3 x 50.8 CM)

"Remember Kurt for what he was: caring, generous, and sweet. Let's keep the music with us. We'll always have it, forever." --- Kristt Novoselic

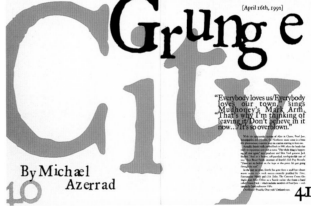

[April 16th, 1991]

Grunge City

"Everybody loves us/Everybody loves our town," sings Mudhoney's Mark Arm, "That's why I'm thinking of leaving it/Don't believe in it now...It's so overblown."

With the spectacular success of Alice in Chains, Pearl Jam, Soundgarden and Nirvana, the Northwest music scene is a hotbed phenomenon, a massive once-in-a-nation catering to bent-over, flannel-heavy twists pushed back to 1985, when the bands that made its reputation were still in town. The whole thing is happening all over again: every producer and their bands, Vinyl guitarists Jack Endino ("And in a heaven, self-parodied, word-splitable sort of way," Steve Power Turtle, vocalist of Seattle's Sub Pop Records. "There are no bodies on the hype at this point. It's just going through the roof."

In the past six years, Seattle has gone from a small but vibrant music scene into a rock musica currently profiled by Time, Entertainment Weekly and USA Today. The Cameron Crowe film Singles stars Matt Dillon as a Seattle rocker who fronts a band called Citizen Dick —which includes members of Pearl Jam — with cameos by local exclusive VIPs.

"Overblown?" Possibly. Over with? Definitely not.

By Michæl Azerrad

10 41

DESIGNER
FRED
WOODWARD
NEW YORK NEW YORK

ART DIRECTOR
FRED
WOODWARD

TYPOGRAPHIC SOURCE
IN-HOUSE

STUDIO
ROLLING STONE

CLIENT
ROLLING STONE

PRINCIPAL TYPE
HISTORICAL
FELL

DESIGNERS
**FRED
WOODWARD AND
LEE BEARSON**
NEW YORK NEW YORK

ART DIRECTOR
**FRED
WOODWARD**

TYPOGRAPHIC SOURCE
IN-HOUSE

STUDIO
ROLLING STONE

CLIENT
ROLLING STONE

PRINCIPAL TYPE
TRIXIE

DIMENSIONS
12 x 20 IN.
(30.5 x 50.8 CM)

xx LifeAfterDeath

xxxx

CourtneyLove
xxxPhotographxx
byMarkSeligerxxx
xxxxxxxxxxxxxxxxx

59 · ROLLING STONE, DECEMBER 15, 1994

DESIGNER
DOUG KEYES
SEATTLE WASHINGTON

LETTERER
DOUG KEYES

TYPOGRAPHIC SOURCE
IN-HOUSE

STUDIO
NBBJ GRAPHIC
DESIGN

CLIENT
EMPTY SPACE
THEATRE

PRINCIPAL TYPES
FRANKLIN
GOTHIC EXTRA
CONDENSED
MODIFIED AND
OCR-B

DIMENSIONS
20 × 26 IN.
(51 × 66 CM)
POSTER

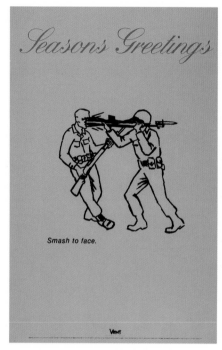

DESIGNERS
TODD FEDELL
AND RUSS HAAN
PHOENIX ARIZONA

TYPOGRAPHIC SOURCE
IN-HOUSE

STUDIO
AFTER HOURS
CREATIVE

CLIENT
VENT

PRINCIPAL TYPE
KÜNSTLER
SCRIPT MEDIUM

DIMENSIONS
24 x 36 IN.
(61 x 91.4 CM)

DESIGNER
PAUL SAHRE
BALTIMORE MARYLAND

TYPOGRAPHIC SOURCE
IN-HOUSE

CLIENT
FELLS POINT
CORNER
THEATRE

PRINCIPAL TYPE
TYPEWRITER

DIMENSIONS
13½ x 20 IN.
(34.3 x 50.8 CM)
POSTER

Fell's Point Corner Theatre

Directed by: Karen Friedland

by: George F. Walker

LOVE and ANGER

Reservations: 276.7837

January 14   February 20

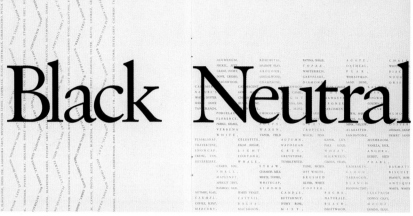

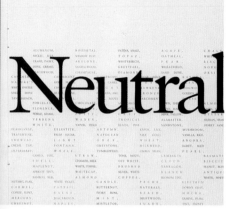

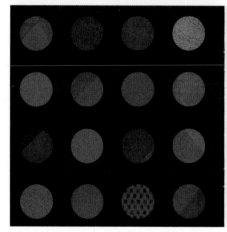

Color can indicate the place in
smooth the way as we go about our daily lives. ¶ Almost as important as the visual is the psychological impli-
which we live. It can imply the
cation of the color compositions around us. Because of the uncertainties of our busy 1990's schedules, we need
types of natural materials we
dependable harmony in our lives, homes and workplaces. This quest leads us to manufacturers and designers
relate to both ethnically and
who can provide us with the option of flexibility — the freedom to move, to change and interchange. ¶
culturally. It is synonymous
Pallas endeavors to offer just that balance. Pallas Textiles, Pallas Walls and Pallas Cases are all collections of
with the distilled demands of
materials designed and colored to envelop you and infuse your life with the spirit of optimism. Thus, as we
our activities in the context of
celebrate the gift of color, we honor its contribution to the story of design throughout the ages...its
the images, trends and current
enhancement of the furniture and furnishings of the interior environment...and the materials that shape them.
design thinking chosen to

Linda Thompson

DESIGNERS
MICHAEL
GERICKE,
DONNA CHING,
AND SHARON
HAREL
NEW YORK NEW YORK
TYPOGRAPHIC SOURCE
IN-HOUSE
STUDIO
PENTAGRAM
DESIGN
CLIENT
PALLAS
TEXTILES
PRINCIPAL TYPE
SABON
DIMENSIONS
7 X 7 IN.
(17.8 X 17.8 CM)

DESIGNER
MICHAEL SKJEI
MINNEAPOLIS
MINNESOTA

TYPOGRAPHIC SOURCE
A.S.A.P.

STUDIO
**M. SKJEI (SHĀ)
DESIGN CO.**

CLIENT
**SHAY, SHEA,
HSIEH & SKJEI,
PUBLISHERS**

PRINCIPAL TYPE
VARIOUS

DIMENSIONS
**6 x 8½ IN.
(15.2 x 21.6 CM)**

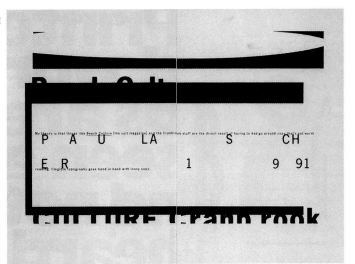

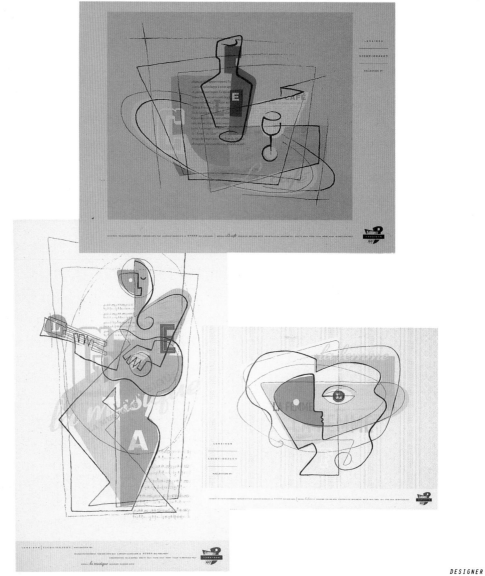

DESIGNER
RÜDIGER GÖTZ
HAMBURG GERMANY

LETTERER
RÜDIGER GÖTZ

TYPOGRAPHIC SOURCE
IN-HOUSE

STUDIO
FACTOR DESIGN

CLIENT
LUNAISON GBR

PRINCIPAL TYPES
ALTERNATE
GOTHIC AND
HANDLETTER-
ING

DIMENSIONS
VARIOUS

DESIGNER
TODD PIPER-
HAUSWIRTH
MINNEAPOLIS
MINNESOTA

ART DIRECTOR
TODD PIPER-
HAUSWIRTH

TYPOGRAPHIC SOURCE
IN-HOUSE

STUDIO
HARD WERKEN •
TEN CATE
BERGMANS
DESIGN BV

CLIENT
HARD WERKEN •
TEN CATE
BERGMANS
DESIGN BV

PRINCIPAL TYPE
20TH CENTURY

DIMENSIONS
8¼ x 11¼ IN.
(21 x 29.2 CM)

PAGE

HARD WERKEN · TEN CATE BERGMANS DESIGN | DITLAAR 1-7 1066 EE AMSTERDAM - SLOTEN | T (31) 020 · 669 44 44

F (31) 020 · 669 31 44

HARD WERKEN

HARD WERKEN · TEN CATE BERGMANS DESIGN BV

DITLAAR 1-7 1066 EE AMSTERDAM - SLOTEN | THE NETHERLANDS

ADRES

TEL · (31) 020 · 669 44 44

FAX · (31) 020 · 669 31 44

● CHRISTINE VAN MOURIK
PROJECT COORDINATOR

graphic · interior · packaging · industrial
exhibit · corporate identity · multi media

design

TE BERGMANS DESIGN

(31) 020 · 669 44 44 | FAX · (31) 020 · 669 31 44

INHOUD:

design | graphic · interior · packaging · industrial · exhibit · corporate identity · multi media

APPLAUD

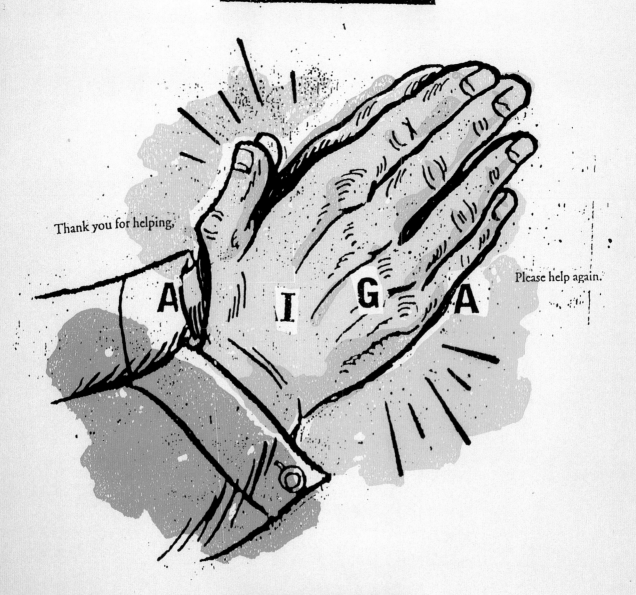

Thank you for helping,

Please help again.

IMPLORE

Paul Sahre 10/100

DESIGNER
PAUL SAHRE
BALTIMORE MARYLAND

TYPOGRAPHIC SOURCE
IN-HOUSE

CLIENT
AMERICAN
INSTITUTE OF
GRAPHIC ARTS/
BALTIMORE
CHAPTER

PRINCIPAL TYPES
BELL GOTHIC
AND ADOBE
GARAMOND

DIMENSIONS
35 x 45 IN.
(88.9 x 114.3 CM)

POSTER

DESIGNER
SHARON WERNER
MINNEAPOLIS MINNESOTA

LETTERER
SHARON WERNER

TYPOGRAPHIC SOURCE
IN-HOUSE

AGENCY
TARGET STORES

STUDIO
WERNER DESIGN
WERKS INC.

CLIENT
TARGET STORES

PRINCIPAL TYPE
TRADE GOTHIC

DIMENSIONS
VARIOUS

PERFORATED

A series of lectures which looks critically at the relationships among contemporary design theory, history and technology.

DESIGNERS
LISA
LAROCHELLE
AND JUREK
WAJDOWICZ
NEW YORK NEW YORK

TYPOGRAPHIC SOURCE
IN-HOUSE

STUDIO
EMERSON,
WAJDOWICZ
STUDIOS, INC.

CLIENT
UNIFEM

PRINCIPAL TYPES
LETTER GOTHIC,
SCHABLONE,
AND AKZIDENZ
GROTESK

DIMENSIONS
8¼ x 11¾ IN.
(21 x 30 CM)

DESIGNER
ANDREW
BLAUVELT
RALEIGH NORTH
CAROLINA

STUDIO
ANDREW
BLAUVELT
GRAPHIC
DESIGN

CLIENT
ATLANTA
COLLEGE OF
ART GALLERY

PRINCIPAL TYPE
FRANKLIN
GOTHIC EXTRA
CONDENSED

DIMENSIONS
22 x 28 IN.
(55.9 x 71.1 CM)

POSTER

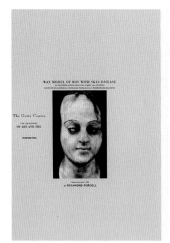

DESIGNERS
NICHOLAS
LOWIE AND
SHERIDAN
LOWREY
VENICE CALIFORNIA

TYPOGRAPHIC SOURCE
IN-HOUSE

STUDIO
LOWIE/LOWREY
DESIGN

CLIENT
THE GETTY
CENTER FOR
THE HISTORY
OF ART AND THE
HUMANITIES

PRINCIPAL TYPES
BODONI,
HELVETICA,
GARAMOND,
GOUDY,
GROTESQUE,
AND CASLON

DIMENSIONS
6¼ x 9 in.
(15.9 x 22.9 CM)

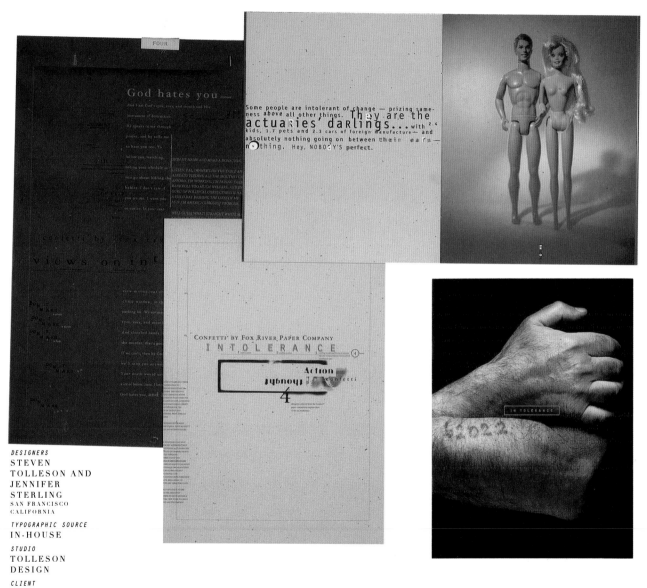

DESIGNERS
**STEVEN
TOLLESON AND
JENNIFER
STERLING**
SAN FRANCISCO
CALIFORNIA

TYPOGRAPHIC SOURCE
IN-HOUSE

STUDIO
**TOLLESON
DESIGN**

CLIENT
**FOX RIVER
PAPER COMPANY**

PRINCIPAL TYPE
GARAMOND

DIMENSIONS
10³/₄ x 15 IN.
(27.3 x 38.1 CM)

184

DESIGNERS
STEFAN NOWAK
AND FONS
HICKMANN
DÜSSELDORF GERMANY

LETTERERS
FONS HICKMANN
AND STEFAN
NOWAK

TYPOGRAPHIC SOURCE
IN-HOUSE

AGENCY
GRAFIKBÜRO

CLIENT
GOD'S
FAVORITE DOG

PRINCIPAL TYPES
SWIFT ONE
AND UNIVERS

DIMENSIONS
5 X 5 1/2 IN.
(12.5 X 14 CM)

DESIGNER
UWE LOESCH
DÜSSELDORF GERMANY

TYPOGRAPHIC SOURCE
IN-HOUSE

CLIENT
DAS
KOM(M)ÖDCHEN
DÜSSELDORF

PRINCIPAL TYPE
AMERICAN TEXT
BT

DIMENSIONS
46 7/8 X 66 1/8 IN.
(119 X 168 CM)

POSTER

regie: horst-gottfried wagner

texte: heinrich pachl,
volkmar staub

musik: heike beckmann,
henning nierstenhöfer

bühne: pit fischer

schnupp: und besch

vorstellungen
dienstag bis freitag 20.30 uhr.
samstag 18.00 und 21.00 uhr.
vorverkauf an den bekannten
konm(m)ödchen-kasse; kunsthalle.
montag bis freitag
11 bis 14 uhr und 16 bis 20 uhr.
samstag ab 14 uhr.
telefon 32 94 43 und 32 54 28

leitung: kay s. lorentz

das kom
kreuzabet für deutschland
und schiller für deutschland
heinrich hambitzer · wolfgang maller

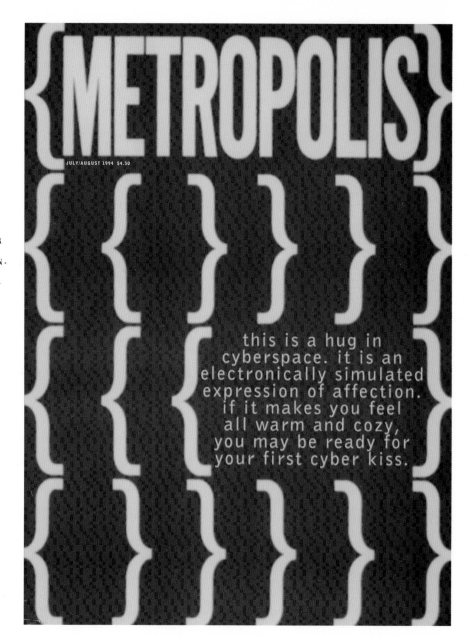

MAGAZINE COVER

186

DESIGNERS
NANCY KRUGER
COHEN AND
CARL LEHMANN-
HAUPT
NEW YORK NEW YORK

TYPOGRAPHIC SOURCE
IN-HOUSE

CLIENT
METROPOLIS
MAGAZINE

PRINCIPAL TYPE
BELL GOTHIC

DIMENSIONS
11 x 15 IN.
(27.9 x 38.1 CM)

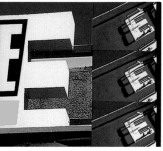

DESIGNER
LAURA PARESKY
LOS ANGELES CALIFORNIA

PHOTOGRAPHER
LAURA PARESKY

TYPOGRAPHIC SOURCE
IN-HOUSE

CLIENT
E! ENTERTAINMENT
TELEVISION

TELEVISION
IDENTITY
CAMPAIGN

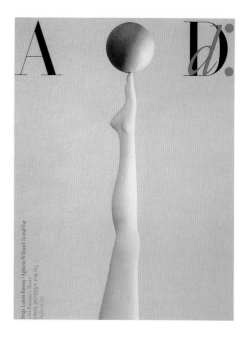

DESIGNER
DAVID KAMPA
AUSTIN TEXAS
LETTERER
DAVID KAMPA
STUDIO
KAMPA DESIGN,
INC.
CLIENT
NIKE

A partir de agora, você vai conhecer o mais importante veículo dirigido ao mundo publicitário, o Advertising Art Director Journal - a *AdD*. lançamento da revista Gráfica/Casa de Idéias editora. A *AdD* vem mexer com o mercado editorial, pelo seu arrojo gráfico, vem para registrar, com profissionalismo e bom gosto, tudo o que se produz no Brasil e no exterior na área de Publicidade e arte Editorial. Colunas internacionais escritas pelos mais renomeados colaboradores de revistas dedicadas à publicidade e design como a Art Direction, Communication Arts, Hot Ads, Directions e Archive, por exemplo, serão reproduzidas na *AdD*. Também, com exclusividade, artigos e portfólios de Diretores de Criação e Diretores de Arte como Leagas Delaney, Bobie Barrie, John Doyle, Larr Bennet, Gary Goldsmith, Cabell Harris, Rich Silvertein, Chery Heller, Tom Lichtenheld, Masatoshi Toda, Tsuguya Inoue, Katsumi Asaba, Mike Gibbs, Bill Miller etc. Ads brasileiros como Paschoal Fabra Neto, Marcello Serpa, Roberto Cippola, Mauro Perez, Marcelo Nepomuceno, Kélio Rodrigues, Hélio de Oliveira, Gabriel Zellmeister, Helga Miethke, entre outros, assim como as cabeças da criação como Ana Carmen Longobardi, Washington Olivetto, Nizan Guanaes, Aurélio Julianelli, Luiz Toledo, etc. Agências então, impossível enumerar pela falta de espaço. A *AdD* publicará artigos com "Cases", um show dos melhores anúncios do mês, publicados no Brasil e no exterior (lado a lado), colunas fixas e os artigos-portfólio do pessoal de arte e fotografia. Uma parte da revista é dedicada à arte editorial, onde predomina a fotografia, mas também a diretores de arte como Fabien Baron (Bazaar), Douglas Lloyd (da nova Mademoiselle ele é o designer dos ads da GAP), Galie Jean-Louis (do caderno cultural Impulse-Daily News), Gary Koepke (da Vibe e World Tour, ex-Ad da Global), Tibor Kalman (que faz Interview e Colors/Benetton) entre tantos outros. Muita, mas muita reprodução de anúncios e matérias especificamente dirigidas ao pessoal de criação é o que predomina, sobretudo, com qualidade gráfica e editorial. Quem conhece o trabalho do Miran e a revista Gráfica, já pode imaginar que qualidade e alto padrão visual serão as virtudes da *AdD*, pra começar.

DESIGNER
OSWALDO
MIRANDA (MIRAN)
CURITABA PRBRAZIL

TYPOGRAPHIC SOURCE
FOTOLASER/
FONTE FOTOCOMP.

STUDIO
CASA DE IDÉIAS

CLIENT
ADD PUBLISHER

PRINCIPAL TYPES
BODONI AND
GARAMOND

DIMENSIONS
$11^{7}/8 \times 8^{1}/2$ IN.
(30 × 21.5 CM)

AdD: Magazine de Arte Publicitária, Ilustração, Fotografia e Arte Editorial.
É muito difícil criar um bom trabalho. É mais difícil ainda vendê-lo. (David Metcalf.

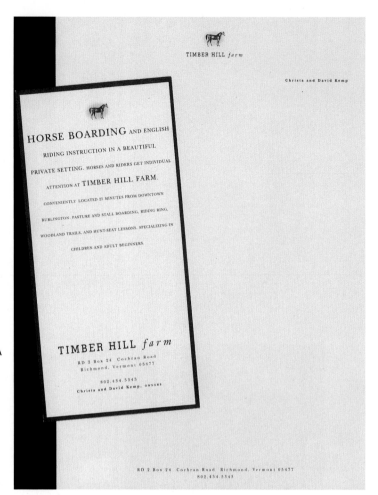

DESIGNER
CHRISTOPHER VICE
BURLINGTON VERMONT

ART DIRECTOR
JANET JOHNSON

CREATIVE DIRECTOR
MICHAEL JAGER

TYPOGRAPHIC SOURCE
IN-HOUSE

STUDIO
JAGER DI PAOLA KEMP DESIGN

CLIENT
TIMBER HILL FARM

PRINCIPAL TYPES
GROTESQUE, BASKERVILLE, MEMPHIS, AND JANSON ITALIC

DIMENSIONS
VARIOUS

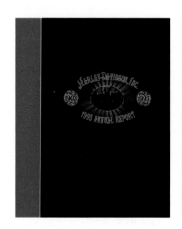

DESIGNER
CURT
SCHREIBER
CHICAGO ILLINOIS

LETTERER
JON YOUSSI

TYPOGRAPHIC SOURCE
IN-HOUSE

STUDIO
VSA PARTNERS,
INC.

CLIENT
HARLEY-
DAVIDSON, INC.

PRINCIPAL TYPES
CLARENDON
AND WALBAUM

DESIGN DIRECTOR
DANA ARNETT

DIMENSIONS
9 x 11 IN.
(22.7 x 27.9 CM)

ANNUAL
REPORT

THE 90TH ANNIVERSARY REUNION

A QUAINT FAMILY GATHERING
HARLEY-DAVIDSON STYLE.

Milwaukee Welcomes Harley Riders

"When I saw all those people waving to us, tears ran down my cheeks. It was kind of embarrassing until I saw the guys riding next to me getting choked up, too."

HAPPY 90TH HARLEY-DAVIDSON

In June of 1993, the eyes of the world looked to Milwaukee, Wisconsin, as Harley-Davidson, the only major American-based motorcycle manufacturer, celebrated its 90th Anniversary. Over 100,000 members of the worldwide Harley-Davidson family answered the call to come home and celebrate 90 years of great American motorcycles.

MUSCULAR DYSTROPHY ASSOCIATION

THE HARLEY-DAVIDSON FAMILY OF EMPLOYEES, DEALERS AND CUSTOMERS HAS RAISED MORE THAN $16 MILLION FOR THE MUSCULAR DYSTROPHY ASSOCIATION IN THE LAST 13 YEARS. 90TH ANNIVERSARY ACTIVITIES RAISED MORE THAN $1 MILLION FOR MDA.

While tens of thousands of riders were motoring toward Wisconsin for the June 12 Reunion, over 22,000 Harley Owners Group members were already in Milwaukee, enjoying the club's 10th Annual Rally. After an emotional parade through downtown Milwaukee, the family arrived at the city's lakefront for the Reunion, an all-day celebration of the Harley-Davidson lifestyle experience. No one left disappointed.

THE REUNION 90 YEARS
MOTOR HARLEY-DAVIDSON COMPANY
1903 ★ 1993

90TH EVENT NETS OVER $1 MILLION FOR MDA

"I was overwhelmed with emotion when our parade was rolling into downtown Milwaukee. I looked up into heaven and told the founding fathers, 'Thanks, guys.'"

"LAST NIGHT I SOLD MY SHIRT FOR $300 FOR MDA. I EVEN SOLD MY BELT BUCKLE ONCE AND HAD TO GO THE REST OF THE DAY WITH A ROPE HOLDING MY PANTS UP."

HARLEY RIDERS SPENT MORE THAN $10 MILLION ON FOOD, GOODS AND SERVICES IN MILWAUKEE. "THOSE OF US WHO WERE HERE WILL NEVER FORGET IT."

Art Center at Night

Art Center at Night, the nondegree program of Art Center College of Design, provides a wide range of courses scheduled conveniently at night and on Saturdays. In keeping with the international reputation of Art Center College of Design, Art Center at Night provides the same high educational standards for part-time students. Those who enroll in Art Center at Night include beginners wanting to investigate creative potential and direction, working professionals seeking to refine their skills or acquire new ones, and artists interested in continuing their education and professional development. Many are future Art Center students who are building a solid foundation in art and design prior to entering the full-time degree program.

SUMMER 1994

ART
CENTER
COLLEGE OF
DESIGN

DESIGNER
DARIN BEAMAN
PASADENA CALIFORNIA

ART DIRECTOR
**REBECA
MÉNDEZ**

PHOTOGRAPHER
**STEVEN A.
HELLER**

TYPOGRAPHIC SOURCE
IN-HOUSE

STUDIO
**ART CENTER
COLLEGE OF
DESIGN –
DESIGN OFFICE**

CLIENT
**ART CENTER
COLLEGE OF
DESIGN**

PRINCIPAL TYPE
LETTER GOTHIC

DIMENSIONS
**12 x 7³/₄ in.
(30.5 x 19.7 cm)**

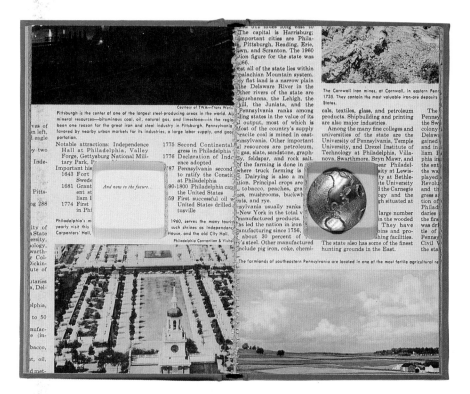

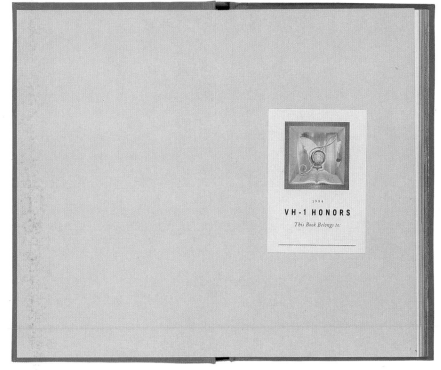

DESIGNER
SHARON
WERNER
MINNEAPOLIS
MINNESOTA

LETTERER
SHARON
WERNER

ART DIRECTOR
CHERI DORR

TYPOGRAPHIC SOURCE
GREAT FACES,
INC.

STUDIO
WERNER
DESIGN WERKS
INC.

CLIENT
VH-1

PRINCIPAL TYPES
TRADE GOTHIC
BOLD, CASLON
ROMAN, AND
CASLON ITALIC

DIMENSIONS
7½ x 4¾ IN.
(19.1 x 12.1 CM)

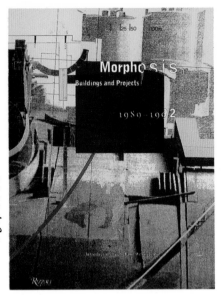

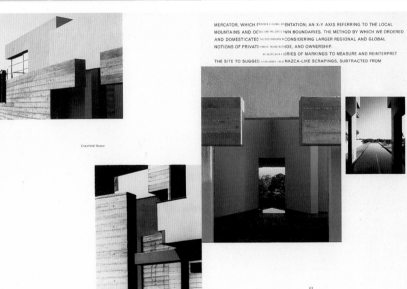

WE BECAME INCREASINGLY INTERESTED IN EVOKING SOME SENSE OF A RELEASE FROM GROUNDEDNESS. THE CONSTRICTED SITE LED US TO PROPOSE LIFTING A CORNER BUILDING OFF THE GROUND TO PRESERVE AN IMPORTANT PEDESTRIAN PATH BORDERING THE SITE. THIS STRUCTURE IS TETHERED TO A SINGLE COLUMN, ALLOWING IT TO ROTATE AND ADJUST TO THE SITE. THIS SOLUTION ARTICULATES THE CORNER AND CREATES A GATEWAY TO THE OLDER CENTRAL CAMPUS BY INCREASING THE BUILDING'S SCALE RELATIVE TO THAT OF THE ADJACENT MCCOSH HALL.

PRINCETON HUMANITIES BUILDING

MERCATOR, WHICH PROVIDES A GLOBAL ORIENTATION; AN X-Y AXIS REFERRING TO THE LOCAL MOUNTAINS AND OCEAN AND THE SITE'S OWN BOUNDARIES. THE METHOD BY WHICH WE ORDERED AND DOMESTICATED THE SITE INVOLVED RE-CONSIDERING LARGER REGIONAL AND GLOBAL NOTIONS OF PRIVATE, PUBLIC, INSIDE/OUTSIDE, AND OWNERSHIP.

WE ALSO DID A SERIES OF MARKINGS TO MEASURE AND REINTERPRET THE SITE TO SUGGEST A RAIN DANCE, THESE NAZCA-LIKE SCRAPINGS, SUBTRACTED FROM

Crawford House

DESIGNERS
LORRAINE WILD,
WHITNEY LOWE,
AND ANDREA
FELLA
LOS ANGELES
CALIFORNIA

TYPOGRAPHIC SOURCE
IN-HOUSE

STUDIO
REVERB

CLIENT
RIZZOLI
INTERNATIONAL
PUBLICATIONS

PRINCIPAL TYPES
HARD TIMES
AND MONOTYPE
GROTESQUE

DIMENSIONS
8½ x 11 IN.
(21.6 x 27.9 CM)

DESIGNER
DAVID CARSON
SAN DIEGO CALIFORNIA

TYPOGRAPHIC SOURCE
IN-HOUSE

STUDIO
**DAVID CARSON
DESIGN**

CLIENT
RAY GUN

PRINCIPAL TYPE
ZAPF DINGBATS

DIMENSIONS
12 x 20 IN.
(30.5 x 50.8 CM)

MAGAZINE
SPREAD

s:Peter Morello stylist: Jill Spector

DESIGNER
CHIP KIDD
NEW YORK, NEW YORK

TYPOGRAPHIC SOURCE
PHOTO-
LETTERING, INC.

STUDIO
CHIP KIDD
DESIGN

CLIENT
ALFRED A.
KNOPF INC.

PRINCIPAL TYPE
BELL GOTHIC
BOLD

DIMENSIONS
6³/₈ X 9¹/₂ IN.
(16.2 X 24.1 CM)

DISCLOSURE

MICHAEL
CRICHTON

DISCLOSURE

A NOVEL

THE SEASON BEGINS OCTOBER 18

THE PUBLIC THEATER

425 Lafayette Street

George C. Wolfe, Producer

BLADE TO THE HEAT
By Oliver Mayer. Directed by George C. Wolfe. Starts Oct. 18. Sexual sparring in and out of the ring. An arresting new play set in the Latin boxing world of the 1950s. $35*

SOME PEOPLE
Written and Performed by Danny Hoch. Directed by Jo Bonney. October 18 - November 13. (In repertory with "The Diva is Dismissed"). Obie-winning solo artist Danny Hoch is your host for a meet-and-greet with some people you'll never forget. $15*

THE DIVA IS DISMISSED
Written and Performed by Jenifer Lewis. Directed by Charles Randolph-Wright. October 27 - November 13 (In repertory with "Some People"). Triple-threat performer Jenifer Lewis takes us on a raucous, raunchy and heart-rending journey through her life and times. $15*

SIMPATICO
Written and Directed by Sam Shepard. Starts November 1. Sam Shepard returns to The Public with a high-stakes look at the daily-double-dealings of two backstabbing businessmen. $35*

THE PETRIFIED PRINCE
A New Musical. Book by Edward Gallardo. Music & Lyrics by Michael John LaChiusa. Choreographed by Rob Marshall. Starts December 6. A ribald new musical from an original screenplay by Ingmar Bergman. $35*

HIM
By Christopher Walken. Directed by Jim Simpson. Starts Dec. 6. ELVIS! Alive and well — and living in limbo. Christopher Walken wrote it, and he'll lead the cast as HIM. $25*

THE MERCHANT OF VENICE
By William Shakespeare. Directed by Barry Edelstein. Starts January 17. The New York Shakespeare Festival celebrates its 40th Anniversary, as Tony-winner Ron Leibman ("Angels in America") exacts a pound of flesh, and the Shakespeare Marathon continues. $35*

A LANGUAGE OF THEIR OWN
By Chay Yew. January. Young, Asian, gay. Lovers become ex-lovers become enemies become friends, in this painfully funny work by a gifted new writer. $25*

SILENCE, CUNNING, EXILE
By Stuart Greenman. Directed by Mark Wing-Davey. February. America, circa 1955. Ike is in. Intellectuals are out. A play suggested by the life of Diane Arbus. $25*

DANCING ON MOONLIGHT
By Keith Glover. March. 20th-century Greek tragedy à la Chester Himes. $25*

DOG OPERA
By Constance Congdon. Directed by Gerald Gutierrez. April. They'd probably be married...if one of them weren't gay. Two people desperate to find in a lover what they've already found in each other. A contemporary comedy about life, love and loneliness in the '90s. $25*

JOIN today and save up to 33% off box office prices! $75 will get you in to 3 shows. $90 will get you 4.
PICK YOUR PLAYS AND DATES LATER — at your convenience. We'll send you performance schedules for each of the plays and you can reserve tickets before they go on sale to the general public.
TICKET HOTLINE: 212-598-7150

HOW TO ORDER
Box Office: 212-598-7150. Daily, after 1 pm to charge to your major credit card. For additional information or a brochure call (Mon. - Fri., 10 am - 5 pm): Ticket Services — 212-598-7115. Groups — 212-598-7107.
(Offer valid through 12/31/94. Subject to availability. Plays, dates and artists subject to change. Single tickets to go on sale later in the season.)
*Single ticket price
Performance Times: Tues., Wed., Thurs., Fri. at 8 pm; Sat. and Sun. at 3 & 8 pm.

BRAVE NEW WORKS, BRAVE NEW WORLDS AND EASY NEW WAYS TO GET IN ON THE GROUND FLOOR.

FROM THE PEOPLE WHO GIVE YOU SHAKESPEARE IN THE PARK

THE PUBLIC THEATER

BLADE TO THE HEAT
SOME PEOPLE
THE DIVA IS DISMISSED
SIMPATICO
THE PETRIFIED PRINCE
HIM
THE MERCHANT OF VENICE
A LANGUAGE OF THEIR OWN
SILENCE, CUNNING, EXILE
DANCING ON MOONLIGHT
DOG OPERA

TICKET HOTLINE: (212) 598-7150

PLAY INFO: SEE OTHER SIDE

DESIGN: PENTAGRAM

DESIGNER
PAULA SCHER
NEW YORK NEW YORK

TYPOGRAPHIC SOURCE
IN-HOUSE

STUDIO
PENTAGRAM DESIGN

CLIENT
THE PUBLIC THEATER

PRINCIPAL TYPES
MORGAN GOTHIC,
PAULAWOOD,
SERIWOOD,
E TEN,
E SEVENTEEN,
E TWENTY-FIVE,
WOOD BLOCK CONDENSED,
AND ALTERNATE GOTHIC NO. 2

DIMENSIONS
VARIOUS

CORPORATE IDENTITY

DESIGNER
MONDREY SIN
HONG KONG

ART DIRECTORS
**STEFEN GRAEFE
AND LAVIN
KWAN**

CREATIVE DIRECTOR
**PAUL
RICHARDSON**

WRITER
ANDREW REZNIK

TYPOGRAPHIC SOURCE
MONDREY SIN

AGENCY
**BATES HONG
KONG**

CLIENT
**BRITISH
AMERICAN
TOBACCO**

PRINCIPAL TYPE
HANDLETTERING

DIMENSIONS
7⁷/₈ x 6⁷/₈ IN.
(20 x 17.5 CM)

DESIGNER
**NINJA V.
OERTZEN**
DUISBURG GERMANY

TYPOGRAPHIC SOURCE
IN-HOUSE

CLIENT
**UNIVERSITÄT
GHS ESSEN,
PROF. VOLKER
KÜSTER**

PRINCIPAL TYPE
BLUR

DIMENSIONS
39³/₈ x 22⁷/₈ IN.
(100 x 58 CM)

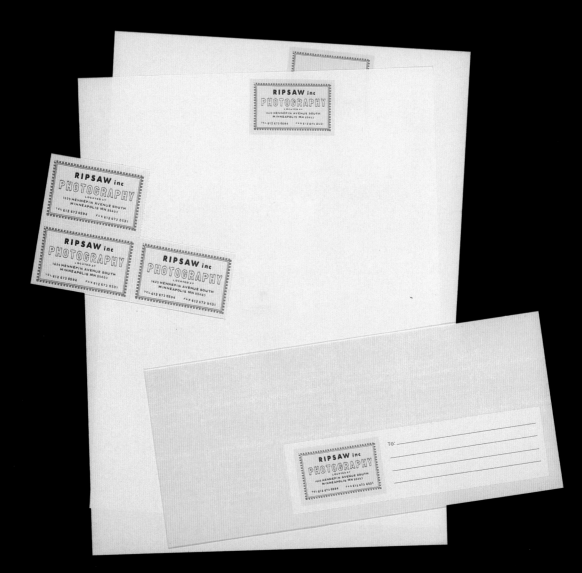

DESIGNER
SHARON
WERNER
MINNEAPOLIS
MINNESOTA

LETTERER
SHARON
WERNER

TYPOGRAPHIC SOURCE
IN-HOUSE

STUDIO
WERNER
DESIGN WERKS
INC.

CLIENT
RIPSAW
PHOTOGRAPHY

PRINCIPAL TYPES
BANK GOTHIC
AND HAND-
LETTERING

DIMENSIONS
8¹/₂ x 11 IN.
(21.6 x 27.9 CM)

DESIGNERS
CHARLES S.
ANDERSON,
JOEL TEMPLIN,
ERIK JOHNSON,
PAUL HOWALT,
AND TODD
PIPER-HAUSWIRTH
MINNEAPOLIS MINNESOTA

ART DIRECTOR
CRAIG TANIMOTO

TYPOGRAPHIC SOURCE
IN-HOUSE

AGENCY
CHIAT DAY
ADVERTISING

CLIENT
NISSAN
PATHFINDER

PRINCIPAL TYPES
TRADE GOTHIC
CONDENSED
AND 20TH
CENTURY

DIMENSIONS
10³/₇ x 16 IN.
(27.3 x 40.6 CM)

Amusing affairs. Rousing

receptions. Sophisticated

soirees. Whatever it is,

rise to the occasion with the

CORDIAL6

refinement of Crane A6.

Open this envelope for a

special look at the right

way to invite attention.

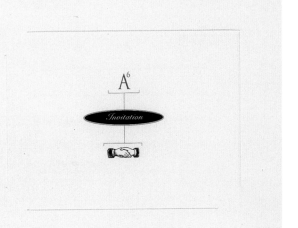

DESIGNER
ERIC MADSEN
MINNEAPOLIS
MINNESOTA

TYPOGRAPHIC SOURCE
IN·HOUSE

DESIGN FIRM
**THE OFFICE OF
ERIC MADSEN**

CLIENT
**CRANE
BUSINESS
PAPERS**

PRINCIPAL TYPES
**BERNHARD
MODERN AND
TRAJAN**

DIMENSIONS
9 x 7 IN.
(22.9 x 17.8 CM)

DESIGNERS
KOBE AND ALAN
LEUSINK
MINNEAPOLIS
MINNESOTA

TYPOGRAPHIC SOURCE
IN·HOUSE

STUDIO
DUFFY DESIGN

CLIENT
PHILLIPS
BEVERAGE
COMPANY

PRINCIPAL TYPES
LETTER
GOTHIC,
GOTHIC 13,
MONOTYPE
SCRIPT BOLD,
SNELL
ROUNDHAND,
AND RALEIGH

PHOTO: DARRELL EAGER
MPLS, MINN.
STUDENT DESIGN CONFERENCE
WEIGHT
TOTAL PRICE
BULK RATE
0 22345 90805 2
ACD-94
SDC-08
*WARNING: A design degree could be hazardous to your financial health.
Every year 1000's of college graduates
compete for only a handful of graphic design jobs.
A C/D CHICAGO
SDC
first
BURN
degree
1994
(ACD-08)
AMERICAN
CENTER FOR DESIGN
•APRIL 15-17
CHICAGO, ILL.
CHARLES S. ANDERSON: KEYNOTE
Design: Charles S. Anderson, Paul Howalt / Copy: Lisa Pemrick / Photography: Darrell Eager / Paper: French Dur-O-Tone Butcher White / Film: LPP Lithocolor / Printing: RFP Enterprises

DESIGNERS
CHARLES S. ANDERSON AND PAUL HOWALT
MINNEAPOLIS MINNESOTA

TYPOGRAPHIC SOURCE
IN-HOUSE

AGENCY
CHARLES S. ANDERSON DESIGN COMPANY

CLIENT
AMERICAN CENTER FOR DESIGN

PRINCIPAL TYPES
20TH CENTURY AND FRANKLIN GOTHIC CONDENSED

DIMENSIONS
24 x 34 IN.
(61 x 86.4 CM)

POSTER

DESIGNER
DARIN BEAMAN
PASADENA CALIFORNIA

CREATIVE DIRECTOR
STUART I. FROLICK

DESIGN DIRECTOR
REBECA MÉNDEZ

TYPOGRAPHIC SOURCE
IN-HOUSE

STUDIO
ART CENTER COLLEGE OF DESIGN – DESIGN OFFICE

CLIENT
ART CENTER COLLEGE OF DESIGN

PRINCIPAL TYPES
MINION, PERPETUA, FRANKLIN GOTHIC, HELVETICA, TEMA CANTANTE, AND LIP

DIMENSIONS
10 x 7 IN.
(25.4 x 17.8 CM)

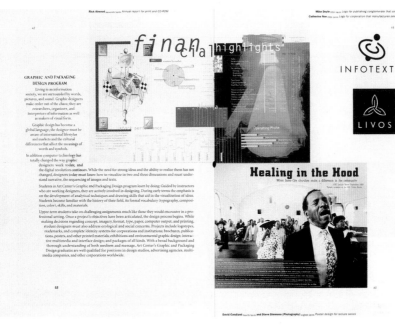

DESIGNER
FRITZ KLAETKE
BOSTON
MASSACHUSETTS

TYPOGRAPHIC SOURCE
IN-HOUSE

STUDIO
**VISUAL
DIALOGUE**

CLIENT
**AMERICAN
INSTITUTE OF
GRAPHIC
ARTS/BOSTON
CHAPTER**

PRINCIPAL TYPE
BEMBO

DIMENSIONS
6¹⁄₄ x 9¹⁄₄ IN.
(15.9 x 23.5 CM)

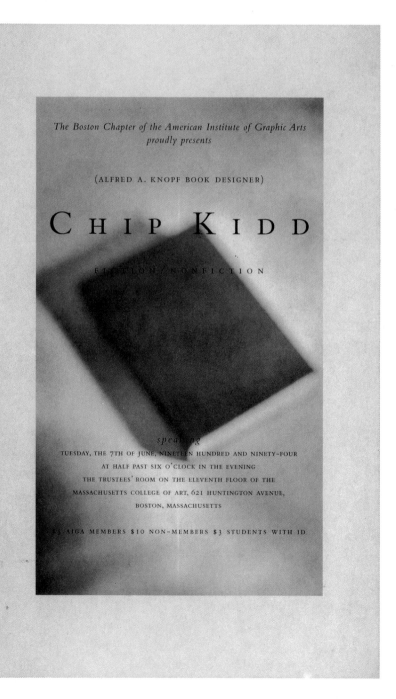

*The Boston Chapter of the American Institute of Graphic Arts
proudly presents*

(ALFRED A. KNOPF BOOK DESIGNER)

CHIP KIDD

FICTION/NONFICTION

speaking
TUESDAY, THE 7TH OF JUNE, NINETEEN HUNDRED AND NINETY-FOUR
AT HALF PAST SIX O'CLOCK IN THE EVENING
THE TRUSTEES' ROOM ON THE ELEVENTH FLOOR OF THE
MASSACHUSETTS COLLEGE OF ART, 621 HUNTINGTON AVENUE,
BOSTON, MASSACHUSETTS

$5 AIGA MEMBERS $10 NON-MEMBERS $3 STUDENTS WITH ID

CF
CF
DA
(1993)
D

THE SNE AK ER

(special award for influence on fashion)

DESIGNER
DOUGLAS
LLOYD
NEW YORK NEW YORK

TYPOGRAPHIC SOURCE
IN-HOUSE

STUDIO
LLOYD (+ CO.)

CLIENT
COUNCIL OF
FASHION
DESIGNERS

PRINCIPAL TYPE
NEWS GOTHIC

DIMENSIONS
10½ x 13½ IN.
(26.7 x 34.3 CM)

"from vreeland's rib came POLLY MELLEN. from that day on, eden never looked better."
—RICHARD AVEDON

(lifetime achievement award)

XLOGIC

In the Tricolour, for example, the white cannot be darker than the blue and red.

Here we have a sort of mathematics of colour.

But pure yellow too is lighter than pure, saturated red, or blue.

And is this proposition a matter of *experience*?

I don't know, I would have to see them. And yet, if I had seen them, I would know the answer once and for all, like the result of an arithmetical calculation.

Where do we draw the line here between logic and experience?

"I feel X, I observe X."

bedient

man bedient sich, um klar zu sehen, oft
rfarbter Brillenglaser, aber nie truber

um klar zu sehen

oft gefardter

Brillenglaser

*man bedient sich, um klar zu sehen, oft
gefarbier, Brillenglaser, aber nie truber*

DESIGNERS
VANCE STUDLEY,
WITH 27 STUDENT
DESIGNS
PASADENA CALIFORNIA

TYPOGRAPHIC SOURCE
IN-HOUSE

STUDIO
ARCHETYPE
PRESS

CLIENT
ART CENTER
COLLEGE
OF DESIGN

PRINCIPAL TYPE
48 FONTS OF
METAL FOUNDRY
TYPE

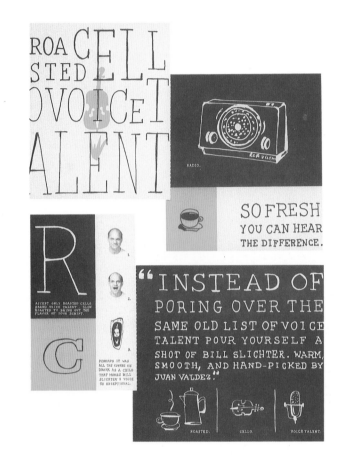

DESIGNER
SHARON WERNER
MINNEAPOLIS MINNESOTA

LETTERER
SHARON WERNER

STUDIO
WERNER DESIGN
WERKS INC.

CLIENT
ROASTED CELLO
VOICE TALENT

PRINCIPAL TYPE
HANDLETTERING

DIMENSIONS
10½ x 12 IN.
(26.7 x 30.5 CM)

DESIGNER
LOUISE FILI
NEW YORK NEW YORK

TYPOGRAPHIC SOURCE
WILD CARROT
LETTERPRESS

STUDIO
LOUISE FILI LTD.

CLIENT
LOUISE FILI LTD.

PRINCIPAL TYPE
BEMBO

DIMENSIONS
4¼ x 6 IN.
(10.8 x 15.2 CM)

LOUISE FILI HAS DESIGNED WELL OVER TWO THOUSAND BOOK JACKETS AND COVERS. While the quantity is impressive, the quality of her typography and the acuity of her art direction has made her one of the most recognized, if not imitated, contemporary book and book jacket designers in America. However, since founding Louise Fili Ltd. in 1989 she has not just limited her talents to editorial design, but rather applied her historical knowledge, typographical skill, and conceptual expertise to the design of logos, identities, menus, labels, packages, posters, promotions, and advertisements. What distinguishes her work? In Fili's hands type is not merely a neutral element, but an expressive form to be artfully constructed into compelling communications. Her book jackets for example, are like miniposters, underscored with typography that is sometimes inspired by the poster's history. Used as a reference point, this historical material is a key to new graphic discoveries.

A HISTORY OF AMERICAN GRAPHIC DESIGN NUMBER FIVE • THE SCHOOL OF VISUAL ARTS

MODERNISM&ECLECTICISM

SATURDAY, FEBRUARY 22ND & SUNDAY, FEBRUARY 23RD, 1992 AT THE LOEWS SUMMIT HOTEL

POSTER, SCHOOL OF VISUAL ARTS

DESIGNER
SARA BERNSTEIN
BROOKLYN NEW YORK

TYPOGRAPHIC SOURCE
IN-HOUSE

STUDIO
**SARA BERNSTEIN
DESIGN**

CLIENT
**CHAMPION
INTERNATIONAL
CORPORATION**

PRINCIPAL TYPE
**ADOBE
GARAMOND**

DIMENSIONS
9 x 9 IN.
(22.9 x 22.9 CM)

CHAMPION

100 YEARS

of

PAPERMAKING

in

HAMILTON,

OHIO

THE BOOK YEARS

THE END OF AN ERA   On July 10, 1931, Peter
Thomson died at the age of 79.

It was no great surprise. Though technically still in
charge, Thomson had been in poor health for some
time and had already begun to hand off responsibility
to his son and successor Alexander. But it was nonethe-
less a shock to everyone in the Champion family.

The local paper extolled him as "one of the great
industrial leaders of America, a
great leader because he possessed
vision, conviction and courage,"
and a man to be counted among
"the captains of industry who have
led this machine age forward and
forward to new triumphs."

"The life of Peter Gibson
Thomson was in fact a romance
of the industrial development
of the Great Miami Valley," the
Journal-News declared. "He had
enjoyed no unusual advantages
and he himself created the op-
portunities which crowned his
life with success. Into his every
relationship in life, Mr. Thomson carried that ideal
which actuated his every action — the ideal of understanding, kindness, service, honest endeavor and
deserved achievement.

An editorial in the same issue offered the following tribute:

Peter G. Thomson was a successful man — successful
by all the means by which success is measured in the
world of industry. But far greater than this material
success was the high esteem engendered by love in the
hearts of his fellow men. THIS WAS HIS GREATER
SUCCESS — THIS INDEED WAS THE REAL
TRIUMPH OF HIS LIFE.

Kenneth Faist, then safety director at the Hamilton
mill, described Thomson's legacy
in more prosaic terms:

For a third of a century the
Champion Coated Paper Company has been building carefully,
solidly for the future. Champion
mills are modern. Acres of tim-
berland with the pulp mill built in
their midst. Champion operates
the largest tanning extract plant in
the world. Lime comes from
Champion lime kiln in Tennessee.
1,150 tons of coal are required a
day as well as water by the mil-
lions of gallons. Trainloads of clay.
60,000 covers producing mills for
Champion covers, thousands of men, human brains.
All of these make a large, strong, fearless organization.

The two passages stand as twin memorials to the
individual and to the business that he had created. Any
man, even one with as exacting a standard of self-
appraisal as Thomson, would have been proud.

*President Calvin Coolidge (center) and
Chief Justice William Taft welcomed
Peter Thomson to Washington in 1925*

forty

GETTING BY
1931–46

I n the decade and a half after Thomson's death,
Champion was in the hands of two sons born and
bred to the paper business. Alexander, who was
president from 1931 to 1935, successfully steered
the company through the Depression. Logan, in charge
from 1935 to 1946, oversaw expansion into Texas and
Georgia and then led Champion as it met the challenges
of wartime production.

By the time Alexander Thomson donned the man-
tle, he had been well trained for the job. His education
in papermaking began in 1896 when he came to the
mill at the age of 17. "An old photograph shows him
in spattered cap and overalls," Reuben Robertson
recounted, "working among the tubs and vats of the
color room: a slender young man, sporting the type of
luxuriant mustache common in that era. His weekly
wage was $6.00, half of which was paid to his mother
for food and lodging."

Thomson worked on several machines in the mill
before moving on to be order clerk, assistant sales
manager, advertising manager, sales manager, and
vice president. Very much his father's son, he was
active in civic affairs, the YMCA, Boy Scouts, and

Chamber of Commerce in particular. He also had a
lifelong interest in forestry and soil conservation. In
1935, four years after having taken the reins and
guided Champion through the worst of the Depression, he retired as president and was named to the
board. His 42-year Champion career would end with
his death in 1939.

THE CRASH   Though the Depression began with the
stock market crash in 1929, it was a year or two before
the ripples reached the mill. According to Ed Bauer,
who started on the calenders in 1928 and retired in
1971 as foreman on the rewinders, "Things slowed
down in the mill about 1931, mostly in the better
grades of paper. At that time, the stores and other cus-

forty-one

Applied Typography/Japan

New Type

Tókyo

TDC

Exhibition

Este artigo apresenta as melhores peças selecionadas nos dois mais importantes anuários do Japão.

DESIGNER
OSWALDO
MIRANDA (MIRAN)
CURITABA PR BRAZIL

CALLIGRAPHER
OSAMU KATAOKA
TOKYO JAPAN

TYPOGRAPHIC SOURCE
FOTOLASER/
FONTE FOTOCOMP.

STUDIO
CASA DE IDÉIAS

CLIENT
ADD PUBLISHER

PRINCIPAL TYPE
FIRMIN DIDOT

DIMENSIONS
11⁷/₈ x 16¹³/₁₆ IN.
(30 x 43 CM)

EDITORIAL

DESIGNER
RUDY T. ZASLOFF
SAN FRANCISCO
CALIFORNIA

LETTERER
RUDY T. ZASLOFF

TYPOGRAPHIC SOURCE
IN-HOUSE

STUDIO
SONY
SIGNATURES
CREATIVE
SERVICES
DEPARTMENT

CLIENT
SPIN DOCTORS

PRINCIPAL TYPE
PRISKA SERIF

DIMENSIONS
7 x 11$\frac{1}{8}$ IN.
(17.8 x 13.7 CM)

TOUR BOOK

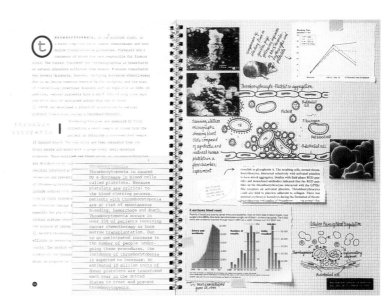

DESIGNERS
**JOHN KLOTNIA,
IVETTE MONTES
DE OCA, AND
WOODY PIRTLE**
NEW YORK NEW YORK

CALLIGRAPHER
**IVETTE MONTES
DE OCA**

TYPOGRAPHIC SOURCE
IN-HOUSE

STUDIO
**PENTAGRAM
DESIGN**

CLIENT
**ARIAD
PHARMACEUTICALS,
INC.**

PRINCIPAL TYPE
COURIER

DIMENSIONS
**8¹/₂ x 11 IN.
(21.6 x 27.9 CM)**

DESIGNER
DAVE WOZNIAK
CHICAGO ILLINOIS

TYPOGRAPHIC SOURCE
IN-HOUSE

DESIGN FIRM
VSA PARTNERS,
INC.

CLIENT
WICKLANDER
PRINTING
CORPORATION

PRINCIPAL TYPES
INTERSTATE,
LETTER GOTHIC,
AND FRANKLIN
GOTHIC

DESIGN DIRECTOR
TED STOIK

DIMENSIONS
6½ x 9 IN.
(16.5 x 22.9 CM)

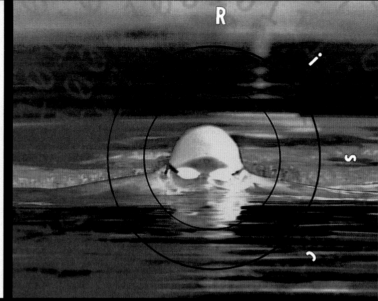

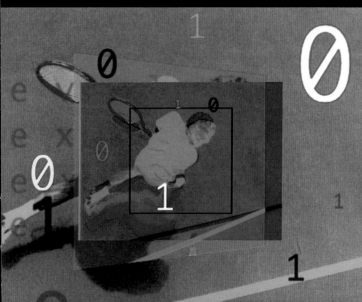

DESIGNERS
CHRISTOPHER
WARGIN AND
DENNIS LIM
HOLLYWOOD
CALIFORNIA

TYPOGRAPHIC SOURCE
IN-HOUSE

AGENCY
BBDO,
LOS ANGELES

STUDIO
CHRISTOPHER
WARGIN

CLIENT
MOTOROLA

PRINCIPAL TYPES
MONACO, FUTURA
CONDENSED
BOLD, AND TOY
TYPE BLOCKS
TELEVISION
COMMERCIAL

DESIGNERS
RÜDIGER GÖTZ
AND OLAF STEIN
HAMBURG GERMANY

LETTERER
RÜDIGER GÖTZ

TYPOGRAPHIC SOURCE
IN-HOUSE

STUDIO
FACTOR DESIGN

CLIENT
PAPIERMÜHLE
GMUND

PRINCIPAL TYPE
BEMBO

DIMENSIONS
VARIOUS

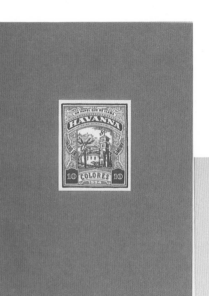

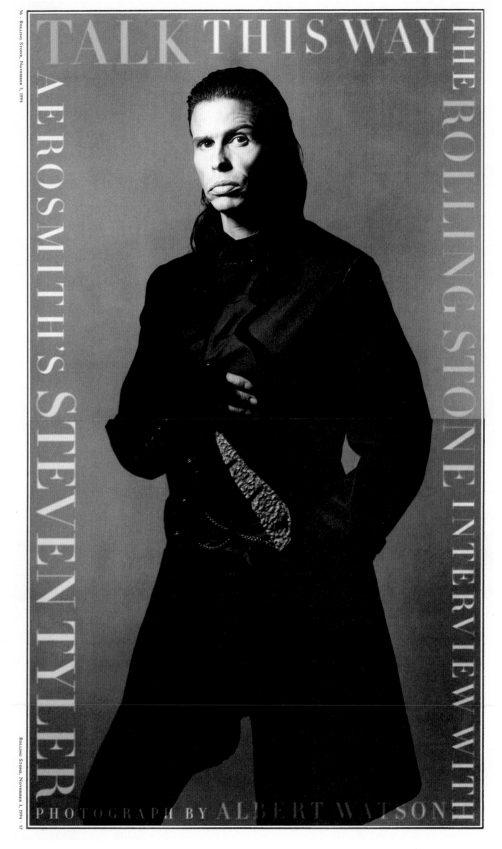

TALK THIS WAY

THE ROLLING STONE INTERVIEW WITH

AEROSMITH'S STEVEN TYLER

PHOTOGRAPH BY ALBERT WATSON

DESIGNERS
FRED WOODWARD
AND GERALDINE
HESSLER
NEW YORK NEW YORK

ART DIRECTOR
FRED WOODWARD

TYPOGRAPHIC SOURCE
IN-HOUSE

STUDIO
ROLLING STONE

CLIENT
ROLLING STONE

PRINCIPAL TYPE
DIDOT

DIMENSIONS
12 × 20 IN.
(30.5 × 50.8 CM)

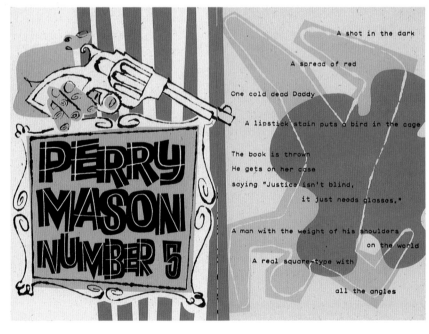

DESIGNERS
CHARLES S.
ANDERSON AND
ERIK JOHNSON
MINNEAPOLIS MINNESOTA

LETTERERS
KAREN BARBOUR
AND ED
FOTHERINGHAM

ART DIRECTOR
CHARLES S.
ANDERSON

ILLUSTRATORS
KAREN BARBOUR
AND ED
FOTHERINGHAM

TYPOGRAPHIC SOURCE
IN-HOUSE

STUDIO
CHARLES S.
ANDERSON
DESIGN COMPANY

CLIENT
FRENCH PAPER
COMPANY

PRINCIPAL TYPES
FRANKLIN
GOTHIC,
GOTHIC 13,
FOTHERINGHAM
SCRIPT, AND
HANDLETTERING

DIMENSIONS
5½ x 8 IN.
(14 x 20.3 CM)

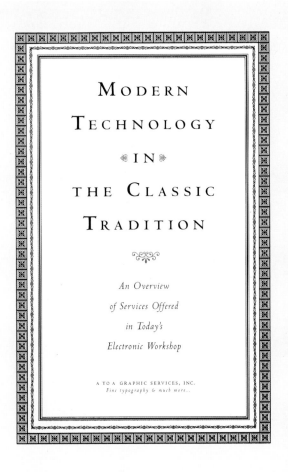

MODERN

TECHNOLOGY

❋ IN ❋

THE CLASSIC

TRADITION

*An Overview
of Services Offered
in Today's
Electronic Workshop*

A TO A GRAPHIC SERVICES, INC.
Fine typography & much more...

Output Hotline

OUR OUTPUT HOTLINE PROVIDES RUN-OUT services to those clients supplying A TO A with Mac or PC disks. Our standard turnaround time for this service is 2–1 hours depending upon the size of the job. Files are generated as laser prints, high resolution RC paper proofs or film (either negatives or positives). For clients seeking electronic color output we offer Tektronix®, Fiery® and Iris® proofs. The Tektronix Phaser III PXi offers an 11 by 17 inch image area plus bleed on any stock (including acetate) from newsprint to 120 lb. text. Iris prints can be ordered with a matte, semi-gloss or gloss finish up to 33 by 44 inches on either Iris

Gone are the days of hand-composed pages being printed on flywheel-driven presses.

[6]

---

paper or acetate. ▥ For those discerning clients, in addition to simply outputting work, we provide file editing, typographic aesthetics and integration of charts, graphs and custom type modifications. These services evolved to meet the ever-growing demands and time constraints faced by graphic arts professionals throughout the Tri-State area, especially on weekends and holidays. ▥ We support the Adobe and Bitstream type libraries as well as type libraries from foundries around the world including Elsner & Flake, Emigré, The Font Bureau, The Font Company, Lanston Type Company, Monotype, and URW. ▥ Files are accepted on any media including floppy disks, SyQuest® cartridges and magneto optical disks. ▥ A Bulletin Board System (BBS) is maintained to allow clients faster service through high-speed digital transmission. The BBS is available 24-hours-a-day, 7-days-a-week. Please call to obtain your user ID and password.

[7]

DESIGNER
ADAM GREISS
NEW YORK NEW YORK

CREATIVE DIRECTORS
**ALLAN R.WAHLER
AND ADAM S.
WAHLER**

TYPOGRAPHIC SOURCE
**A TO A GRAPHIC
SERVICES, INC.**

STUDIO
**ADAM GREISS
DESIGN**

CLIENT
**A TO A GRAPHIC
SERVICES, INC.**

PRINCIPAL TYPES
**MONOTYPE
CENTAUR AND
WOODTYPE
ORNAMENTS**

DIMENSIONS
6¼ x 9 IN.
(15.9 x 22.9 CM)

DESIGNERS
CHRIS WARE AND
CHIP KIDD
CHICAGO ILLINOIS AND
NEW YORK NEW YORK

CALLIGRAPHER
CHRIS WARE

STUDIO
ACME NOVELTY,
INC. WITH CHIP
KIDD DESIGN

CLIENT
NEW YORK ART
DIRECTORS
CLUB

PRINCIPAL TYPE
HANDLETTERING

DIMENSIONS
4 x 5⁷/8 IN.
(10.2 x 14.9 CM)

Reverb. In physics, it refers to the reflection of sound waves in a confined space. As the sound echoes and re-echoes, it modulates and grows louder.

Imagine a hall of mirrors in which everything reflects back on itself. And as the reflections and refractions continue, the originals are gradually drowned in the maelstrom.

Now imagine living in a cyclone of signs, in which signs beget more signs, until the things that generated the signs in the first place are lost.

In effect, reverberation is the polar opposite of recycling–or rather, its demented cousin. For in recycling, something that is original is cherished, preserved, and renewed–while in reverberation, it is distorted and devoured.

So what does that say about those of us in the business of generating signs? Will we embrace the values expressed by recycling–preserving, and honoring, original meanings in some way? Or will we merely be–reverb units?

And if so–how soon before we reach a point of critical mass? How soon before the whole system shatters–in a paroxysm similar to nervous break-

downtown man loves you in the crash on the fifth lap, shocking the spectators and killing the photographer

and your pensive TV knob's got a 20 body fat on the freeway; starve for the avocado newspapers, shotgun

DESIGNER
GARY KOEPKE
MAGNOLIA
MASSACHUSETTS

TYPOGRAPHIC SOURCE
IN-HOUSE

AGENCY
THE KUESTER
GROUP

STUDIO
KOEPKE
INTERNATIONAL,
LTD.

CLIENT
POTLATCH
CORPORATION

PRINCIPAL TYPE
TIMES

DIMENSIONS
7 X 11 IN.
(17.8 X 27.9 CM)

Named one of the top U.S. Companies to work for in *The*
100 Best Companies to Work for in America, Herman Miller
has been a design leader for decades. (But is it fun to work
there?) Under the leadership of creative director Stephen
Frykholm (He's a real gas!), the team at Herman Miller has
helped the company win awards like the AIGA Design
Leadership and Fortune & American Center for Design
Beacon Award. The NY Art Director's Club, CA, Graphis
ID, and AIGA Communication Graphics have also recognized Herman Miller's graphic design. (Some of these
awards are really cool.) Herman Miller offers an attractive
beginning designer's salary (not great, but enough to pay
the rent). Interested candidates holding a BFA or MFA
degree (and a lively imagination) may apply by sending a
maximum of twenty slides of recent work and a resume by
June, 1994. Please include educational and work experience references. (Don't worry, young designers getting the
job before you didn't have much either.) Send resumes to
Herman Miller Inc., Staffing department 0162, PO Box
302, Zeeland, Michigan 49464-0302. (Don't try to buck
the system by sending your stuff directly to Steve. He'll lose
it.) Include a self-addressed, stamped envelope for return
of slides; please do not send actual portfolios. Selected candidates will be contacted by August, 1994 to arrange inter-
views. (We'll buy lunch and give you the real low-down.

DESIGNER
YANG KIM
ZEELAND MICHIGAN

TYPOGRAPHIC SOURCE
IN-HOUSE

CLIENT
HERMAN
MILLER, INC.

PRINCIPAL TYPES
MANIPULATED
ITC BERKELEY
AND HELVETICA
NEUE

DIMENSIONS
25 X 25 IN.
(63.5 X 63.5 CM)

DESIGNER
ANDRÉAS
NETTHOEVEL
BIEL SWITZERLAND

TYPOGRAPHIC SOURCE
IN-HOUSE

STUDIO
SECOND FLOOR
SOUTH

CLIENT
SCHWEIZER
REISEKASSE
(REKA), PETER
LUGINBÜHL

PRINCIPAL TYPES
MARTEN AND
UNIVERS ITALIC

DIMENSIONS
35⅝ x 106⅞ IN.
(90.5 x 271.5 CM)

DESIGNER
CHIP KIDD
NEW YORK NEW YORK
LETTERER
CHIP KIDD
TYPOGRAPHIC SOURCE
PHOTO-
LETTERING,
INC.
STUDIO
CHIP KIDD
DESIGN
CLIENT
ALFRED A.
KNOPF, INC.
PRINCIPAL TYPE
HELVETICA
HEAVY ITALIC
DIMENSIONS
12¼ x 8½ IN.
(31.1 x 21.6 CM)

DESIGNERS
CHARLES S.
ANDERSON AND
PAUL HOWALT
MINNEAPOLIS
MINNESOTA
ART DIRECTOR
CHARLES S.
ANDERSON
TYPOGRAPHIC SOURCE
IN-HOUSE
STUDIO
CHARLES S.
ANDERSON
DESIGN
COMPANY
CLIENT
FRENCH PAPER
COMPANY
PRINCIPAL TYPES
TRADE GOTHIC,
20TH CENTURY,
AND GOTHIC 13
DIMENSIONS
18¾ x 24¼ IN.
(47.6 x 61.6 CM)
POSTER

AGDA + raleigh paper company
(australia presents)

ON A ROLL
With Charles S.
ANDERSON &
JERRY FRENCH

8
1
dn

B66-51

—FROM THE USA TO YOU

AGDA·94
CROSS COUNTRY
DESIGN TOUR

FREE
DOOR PRIZES

Charles S. Anderson
C.S.A. DESIGN COMPANY

SYDNEY	BRISBANE	MELBOURNE
14th June '94, 6.30 pm	16th June 1994, 6.30 pm	20th June, 6.30 pm
Powerhouse Museum,	Royal Aust. Inst. Architects,	Telecom Centre,
500 Harris St., Ultimo	70 Merivale St., S. Brisbane	242 Exhibition St.

W/Special Guest Jerry French

PRESIDENT FRENCH PAPER CO.

· C.S. ANDERSON DESIGN specializes in product design & development, identity, and package design.

Charles S. Anderson started his own design firm in 1989, and has worked with clients including the French Paper Company, Paramount Pictures, Nike, Fossil, Watches, Levis, MTV and Turner Network Television. The firm has designed and

DESIGNER
LOUISE FILI
NEW YORK NEW YORK

TYPOGRAPHIC SOURCE
IN-HOUSE

STUDIO
LOUISE FILI
LTD.

CLIENT
CHRONICLE
BOOKS

PRINCIPAL TYPES
NICOLAS
COCHIN BOLD
AND
CARABINIERI

DIMENSIONS
5¼ x 6⅜ IN. (13.3 x 16.2 CM)

OUTSIDE:IN

DESIGNERS
HERMAN DYAL
AND JOEL
PHILLIPS
AUSTIN TEXAS

TYPOGRAPHIC SOURCE
IN-HOUSE

AGENCY
FULLER DYAL
& STAMPER

CLIENT
TEXAS FINE
ARTS
ASSOCIATION

PRINCIPAL TYPES
DISTURBANCE,
ADOBE
GARAMOND, AND
FRANKLIN
GOTHIC

DIMENSIONS
9 x 6 IN.
(22.9 x 15.2 CM)

Outsider
and Conte
mmporary
Artists in
Texas

DESIGNER
ANTONY
REDMAN
SINGAPORE

ART DIRECTOR
ANTONY
REDMAN

CREATIVE DIRECTOR
JIM AITCHISON

WRITER
ANTONY
REDMAN

TYPOGRAPHIC SOURCE
IN-HOUSE

AGENCY
BATEY ADS
SINGAPORE

CLIENT
HUMANIST
ASSOCIATION
OF HONG KONG

PRINCIPAL TYPE
GOTHIC 13

DIMENSIONS
30¹/₃ x 20¹/₁₆ IN.
(77 x 51 CM)

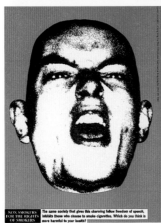

DESIGNER
ROBYNNE RAYE
SEATTLE WASHINGTON

LETTERER
ROBYNNE RAYE

TYPOGRAPHIC SOURCE
IN-HOUSE

STUDIO
MODERN DOG

CLIENT
BARBEAU AND
REV. BOB JONES M.S.

PRINCIPAL TYPE
STENCIL
(HAND DONE)

DIMENSIONS
15 x 23 IN.
(38.1 x 58.4 CM)

DESIGNERS
**EMILIO GIL
CERRACÍN AND
JORGE GARCÍA**
MADRID SPAIN

TYPOGRAPHIC SOURCE
IN-HOUSE

STUDIO
TAU DISEÑO

CLIENT
**ESPAÑA
ABIERTA/OSBORNE**

PRINCIPAL TYPE
DIDOT LH ROMAN

DIMENSIONS
**12 x 12 IN.
(30.5 x 30.5 CM)**

un toro negro y enorme

El Toro Osborne: marca, símbolo, tótem, imagen universal.

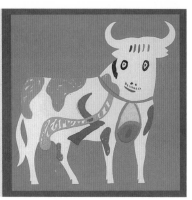

DESIGNER
DAVID CARSON
SAN DIEGO CALIFORNIA

TYPOGRAPHIC SOURCE
IN-HOUSE

STUDIO
DAVID CARSON
DESIGN

CLIENT
RAY GUN

PRINCIPAL TYPE
TEENAGER

DIMENSIONS
12 x 20 IN.
(30.5 x 50.8 CM)

DESIGNERS
**STACY DRUMMOND,
JEFFREY KEYTON,
AND TRACY
BOYCHUK**
NEW YORK NEW YORK

TYPOGRAPHIC SOURCE
IN-HOUSE

AGENCY
**MTV OFF-AIR
CREATIVE**

CLIENT
**MTV:MUSIC
TELEVISION**

PRINCIPAL TYPES
**MARLOW I
AND MARLOW II**

DIMENSIONS
**10½ x 10½ IN.
(26.7 x 26.7 CM)**

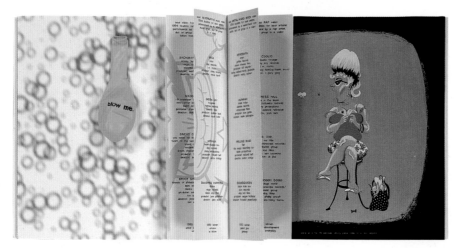

RICK MOODY

AUTHOR OF THE ICE STORM

RICK MOODY

AUTHOR OF THE ICE STORM

HEAVEN

ANGELS AROUND

THE RING OF BRIGHTEST

LITTLE, BROWN

DESIGNER
DAVID HIGH
PUTNAM VALLEY
NEW YORK

TYPOGRAPHIC SOURCE
IN-HOUSE

STUDIO
HIGH DESIGN

CLIENT
LITTLE, BROWN
AND COMPANY
PUBLISHERS

PRINCIPAL TYPES
INTERSTATE BOLD
CONDENSED AND
INTERSTATE
REGULAR
CONDENSED

DIMENSIONS
19 3/8 x 8 1/2 IN.
(49.9 x 21.6 CM)

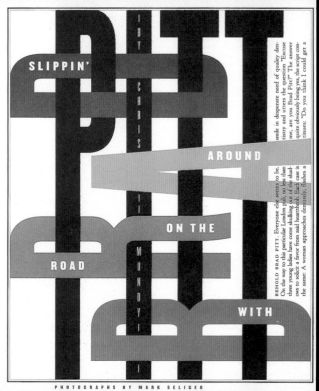

SLIPPIN' [BY CHRIS MUNDY] AROUND ON THE ROAD WITH BRAD PITT

BEHOLD BRAD PITT. Everyone else seems to be. On the way to this particular London pub, no less than three young ladies have come skulking out of the shadows to solicit a favor from said heartthrob. Each case is the same: A woman approaches demurely, flashes a smile in desperate need of quality dentistry and utters the question "Excuse me, are you Brad Pitt?" The answer quite obviously being yes, the script continues: "Do you think I could get a

92 · ROLLING STONE, DECEMBER 1, 1994

PHOTOGRAPHS BY MARK SELIGER

DESIGNER
FRED
WOODWARD
NEW YORK NEW YORK

ART DIRECTOR
FRED
WOODWARD

TYPOGRAPHIC SOURCE
IN-HOUSE

STUDIO
ROLLING STONE

CLIENT
ROLLING STONE

PRINCIPAL TYPE
CHAMPION
GOTHIC

DIMENSIONS
12 × 20 IN.
(30.5 × 50.8 CM)

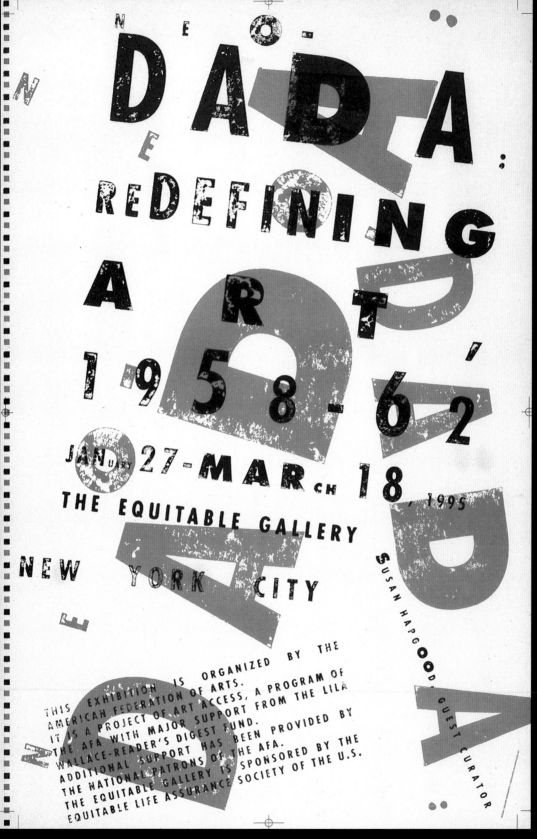

DESIGNER
TAKAAKI
MATSUMOTO
NEW YORK NEW YORK

TYPOGRAPHIC SOURCE
RUBBER STAMP

STUDIO
MATSUMOTO
INCORPORATED

CLIENT
THE EQUITABLE
GALLERY

PRINCIPAL TYPE
GOTHIC

DIMENSIONS
25 × 36 IN.
(63.5 × 91.4 CM)

von der heydt museum
wuppertal
18. dezember 1994 bis
12. februar 1995
örtlich zeitlich persönlich
künstler und gestalter der
bergischen universität
wuppertal :
michael badura
bazon brock
wolfgang körber
uwe loesch
ulrich reif
ursula wevers

DESIGNER
UWE LOESCH
DÜSSELDORF GERMANY
TYPOGRAPHIC SOURCE
IN-HOUSE
CLIENT
VON DER HEYDT
MUSEUM
WUPPERTAL
PRINCIPAL TYPE
SYNTAX BLACK
DIMENSIONS
46$\frac{7}{8}$ X 66$\frac{1}{8}$ IN.
(119 X 168 CM)

DESIGNER
KATRIN
SCHMITT-TEGGE
NEW YORK NEW YORK

CREATIVE DIRECTOR
STEPHEN DOYLE

TYPOGRAPHIC SOURCE
IN-HOUSE

STUDIO
DRENTTEL
DOYLE PARTNERS

CLIENT
COOPER-HEWITT
NATIONAL
DESIGN MUSEUM,
SMITHSONIAN
INSTITUTION

PRINCIPAL TYPE
SABON

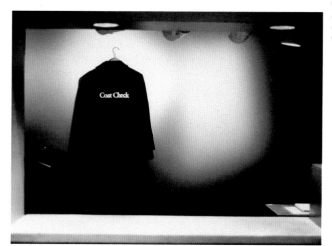

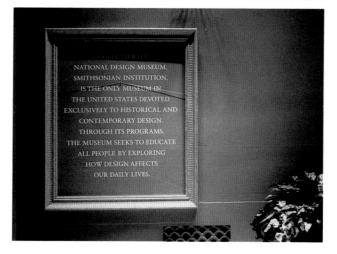

SPREAD
"RUMORS"

PROPAGATE
"LIES"

DESIGNERS
HAL
WOLVERTON
AND ALICIA
JOHNSON
PORTLAND OREGON

TYPOGRAPHIC SOURCE
IN-HOUSE

AGENCY
JOHNSON &
WOLVERTON

CLIENT
AMNESTY
INTERNATIONAL

PRINCIPAL TYPE
DIN
MITTELSCHRIFT

DIMENSIONS
4¹/₂ x 6 IN.
(11.4 x 15.3 CM)

Governments around the world consider supporters of human rights to be dangerous enemies. Dangerous governments try to discredit them — and minimize the importance of human rights abuses. Amnesty itself, which was founded in 1961, was called "one of the larger lunacies of our time."

Violators of human rights think they can intimidate or torture or "disappear" those who dare to differ with them. They believe their crimes will go unnoticed. In some countries just printing a newsletter about government's abuse or neglect of basic human rights is considered to be a punishable act.

But that's not how it has to be. No government likes to be shamed in front of the world. If enough people find out about these abuses and act against them, they will stop. A Salvadoran official is quoted as saying "if there is a lot of pressure — like from Amnesty International or some foreign countries — then we might pass them on to a judge, but if there is no pressure then they're dead."

BE A
"TERRORIST"

We can make waste cheaper to manufacture, can't... waste ... So please recycle this holiday season. It'll be music to everyone's ... son's greetings ... s for the Environm...

In Minnesota, the Saint Paul Pioneer Press used waste to make this newspaper. We used the newspaper to make a holiday greeting. Now it's up to you:

Folick will stay in California

Jeff Folick, president and CEO of HMO PacifiCare Health Systems, has decided against coming to Minnesota as president of health plan operations for United HealthCare. Folick cited family relocation as a major factor. **2F**

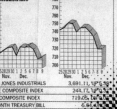

Mortgage rates

FHA-VA	9%	Points: 1 to 1⅞ or more
CONVENTIONAL	9%	Points: ¾ to 1⅞ or more
JUMBO	9%	Points: 1¼ to 2 or more

• 30-year, fixed-rate loans from 20 Twin Cities lenders compiled at 3 p.m. yesterday by independent mortgage adviser Roger Harrington.

H.B. Fuller

Close: **$28**
Down $2.25

Summary: St. Paul-based H.B. Fuller on Thursday said, for the third time since August, that it will raise prices. It cited rising raw material prices. The stock dropped 5.5 percent Thursday and continued the fall Friday, losing $2.25 a share, 8 percent, to close at $28, on volume of 209,600 shares.
Market wrap-up, Page 2F

RETAILING

Entertainment centers planned at two malls

BY ... McCARTNEY STAFF WRITER

Soon Maplewood Mall and Burnsville Center, like the Mall of America, will be able to boast about being a "place for fun in your life."

A family entertainment center called Jumpin' Jax will be the largest tenant at two regional malls besides the anchor department stores, which own their own space. Work began recently on 12,000-square-foot centers in the two malls, and they should be ready to open in early February.

Jumpin' Jax, which is riding the trend toward entertainment in retailing, will feature everything from "2½ football fields" of chutes, ladders and tunnels, to the latest laser tag and virtual reality games for older children, said David ... well, president of Jumpin' Jax.

The center is designed to be secure enough to allow adults to leave their children for up to three hours while they do their shopping.

Customers will pay an admittance fee, ranging from $3 to $5, depending on the counts they have ... they plan ... Children are never ... wear a bar ... coded bracelet, and ... be able to leave without checking ... with staff member. Also, parents ... given pagers in case they are ... at ... they ... shopping at the mall.

"We will have a sophisticated security system — everyone will be scanned ...," Powell said. "No one will leave without the proper guardian."

JAX CONTINUED ON 2F

RESTAURANTS

Trade center losing Favore to build skyway

... KAHN STAFF WRITER

Removing any barrier to a smooth, ... critical, connection to the Children's Museum, the owners of the World Trade Center will close a full-service Italian restaurant on the center's third floor to make way for construction of a skyway.

Favore, which opened three years ago, will close Dec. 31 to assure that a skyway connection to the museum will be completed in time for the museum's scheduled September opening.

The skyway will be built in an area ... it is currently Favore's kitchen. Architects tried to redesign the floor plan to ... the restaurant, but found there was no ... practical way, said Rich Forslund, general manager of Brookfield Development's St. Paul holdings.

Brookfield, based in Toronto, and ... Financial, based in ... recently own the restaurant and the entire World Trade Center. Forslund ... to make a ... restaurant was not being closed because ... poor patronage, and that, indeed, ... sales at the restaurant have grown appreciably since its opening."

But the restaurant's importance pales when compared to good access to the museum, which is under construction at Wabasha and Seventh streets in downtown St. Paul, Forslund said. The center had economic problems similar to ... of downtown St. Paul, and it is counting on the museum to generate a great deal of pedestrian traffic through its skyway. The museum will not have food service.

Forslund said the center's retail space is 78 percent occupied, but that the coming of the museum has sparked interest from potential tenants. Two are in serious discussion with Brookfield and two others are in preliminary stages, he said.

SATURDAY MEMO

T.G.I. Vendredi's

Heard on the street

"Ma chere, let us saunter down to the auberge for some ... Buffalo wings and 'skins!'"

T.G.I. Friday's, the casual dinner chain owned by Carlson Cos., picked ... location ... first restaurant in Paris ... Blvd. Montmartre in Paris.

Wallace Doolin, president of the Dallas-based restaurant chain, and Laurent Civille, director of the Paris restaurant, were on hand when the doors opened to the public on Tuesday.

So who were the restaurant's first customers? Gary Wittredge and Sheila Fowler, tourists from Houston, Texas, wandered in the door to become the Paris site's first patrons.

With Paris and a recent restaurant opening in Manila, Philippines, Carlson Cos. now has 36 T.G.I. Friday's outside the U.S. among its 320 sites. The company says its target is to have 200 international sites by the end of the decade.

Doolin says national cultures will influ...

HEALTH CARE

Psychiatric institute fires 2 in inquiry

Billing practices draw a federal investigation

JUDITH YATES BORGER STAFF WRITER

A four-month internal investigation into billing practices at the Minneapolis Psychiatric Institute has led to the dismissal of its manager and one psychologist.

Allina Health System, which owns the institute, two weeks ago gave the results of its inquiry to Assistant U.S. Attorney Janet Newberg, who is conducting a federal investigation, according to Allina General Counsel Mark Mishek.

Allina dismissed Rick Palmisano, clinic manager; and Jonathan Hoistad, a psychologist, on Dec. 2. Hoistad referred questions to his attorney, David Gaiser, who could not be reached for comment. Palmisano could not be reached either.

Allina also relieved psychiatrist Jean ...

Federal authorities were called in because the complaint related to billing for Medicare and Medical Assistance reimbursements, which are federally financed.

Newberg could not be reached for comment and Mishek declined to discuss the specific cause for dismissal because of the ongoing federal investigation. Allina is cooperating fully with the investigation, Mishek said.

M. Lewis Jr. of his management responsibilities. Lewis' attorney, James Ryan, ... declined to comment other than to say Lewis is unsure of his current association with the institute.

• Minneapolis Psychiatric Institute, housed at Abbott Northwestern Hospital in Minneapolis, employs 11 psychiatrists, six psychologists and three nurses.

> **Minneapolis Psychiatric Institute employs 11 psychiatrists, six psychologists and three nurses.**

No one else is implicated in the investigation at all," said Gloria O'Connell, media relations manager for Abbott.

Allina's investigation was sparked by a specific complaint regarding billing filed by an employee, according to Mishek.

Although the U.S. attorney's investigation involves only Medicare and Medical Assistance reimbursement, the billing complaint is clearly applicable to all third-party payers, Mishek said.

In addition to Medica, a division of Allina, Blue Cross-Blue Shield of Minnesota reimburses doctors for mental health care provided at Minneapolis Psychiatric Institute. The Blues are unaware of any investigation into the institute's billing practices, according to spokesman Karl Oestreich.

U.S. apples may threaten Japan's market

Imports could bring up to 30 ... prices

... LANDERS ASSOCIATED PRESS

... apple of farmer Ku... ... perfect — and ... picked ... shoppers in Tokyo willing ... for a single flawless fruit.

Here, have one," Saito said, proffering the juicy halves of a red Fuji apple.

But along with the chill blasts from Siberia that signal the end of autumn harvest, a new wind is blowing for Japan's apple growers.

Beginning next month, apples from Washington state will go on sale in Japan. And that could change the way of life in Hirosaki, 360 miles north of Tokyo, Japan's self-proclaimed "apple hometown."

Japanese farmers have been growing apples in this ... northern valley since ... seeds were brought ... means ...

"Over ... it has become almost ... ," ... painstakingly remove ... ... to prune ... life trees; little bags are ... and every apple to ensure ... seedless and prevent little nicks caused by brushing against branches in the wind.

Naturally, perfection has its price. A bargain bag of six apples in Tokyo costs around $6. A perfect specimen of an expensive variety like the Mutsu — a gorgeous pale-red giant weighing more than a pound — can go for $6 apiece at a fancy department store.

This is Japanese culture," said Tokuei Kimura, president of the Aomori Apple Association. Japanese consumers, he ...

Masako Saito, wife of apple farmer ..., plucks a Fuji apple from their plot in Hirosaki, Japan's self-proclaimed "apple hometown." U.S. apples will go on sale in Japan ... threaten the Japanese farmers.

... ... want ... with scratches ... uneven color even ... less tasty ... ... just beginning to recover ... a deep recession, consumers have ... counted much more receptive ... counted goods. Even with ...

APPLES CONTINUED ON 2F

DEVELOPMENT

Viacom scuttles plans to build entertainment, sports complex

JOHN PACENTI ASSOCIATED PRESS

... Viacom Inc. on Friday ... ... to build Blockbuster Park ... entertainment ... complex ... eastern edge of the ...

The park would ... to two pro sports ... buster Entertainment ... Wayne Huizenga ... had been pro ... environmental ... nearby wetlands.

The decision ... after Blockbuster ... com, which said the ... ment complex did not fit ...

The company cited the project's high financial and management costs and a complex regulatory process that involved two counties and the city of Miramar.

"Personally, I'm disappointed the pro...

Viacom Inc. on Friday ... to build Blockbuster Park ... appreciate the broader strategic context for this decision."

Viacom has about $10 billion in debt after buying Blockbuster and Paramount Communications Inc. this year. To pare down that debt, the company is selling Madison Square Garden in New York and ... cable TV systems.

... has been speculation for weeks ... Viacom would not proceed with the ... H. Arthur Teele, chairman of the ... County Commission, had said earlier ... that the park was not dead. He ... it would immediately return phone calls.

... plans for Blockbuster Park included ... sports arenas, a theme park, film and music studios, a virtual reality amusement center, theaters, restaurants and retail stores.

The NHL's Florida Panthers and major league baseball's Florida Marlins — both owned by Huizenga — would have played their home games there. There was also ...

FINANCIAL CRISIS

Orange County bond default raises alarms

ROB W... ASSOCIATED PRESS

Orange County's fiscal crisis took an ominous turn after the county missed a ... payment. The day ... million ... and rais... ... the possibility of a domino-style default that could spread much wider financial pain.

Though the size of the payment was relatively small, regulators and market analysts expressed alarm Friday because the big Southern California county had sought bankruptcy protection three days earlier partly to avoid such a step.

"The message by not meeting the pension bond obligations, is it's serious for everyone," said Jon Schotz of Saybrook Capital Corp., a Los Angeles investment banking firm.

Additional defaults would further tarnish the county's sullied financial reputation and hurt the thousands of individual investors who own Orange County municipal bonds and securities.

A number of the bonds have special insurance to continue payments in the event of default. But analysts were focusing on about 30 separate uninsured bond issues totaling about $2 billion.

In other developments in the financial crisis, Merrill Lynch & Co. said it had received a subpoena from the Securities and Exchange Commission over its work for Orange County. Merrill created some of the volatile securities in the troubled investment fund and served as underwriter for a $600 million note issue that enabled the county to buy the securities.

"The subpoena requests information on a variety of matters related to Orange County," said Merrill spokesman Paul Kriphchlow. "We are cooperating fully and providing the information requested."

The debacle began last week when the $20 billion Orange County investment fund revealed it dropped $1.5 billion in value due to the effect of rising interest rates on bonds and complex securities purchased with heavy borrowings. Also snagged in the crisis are 185 local government agencies, including school districts, which invested in the fund.

The county sought Chapter 9 bankruptcy protection for the fund on Tuesday as major Wall Street brokerage firms demanded cash or securities to shore up loan agreements. It was the biggest municipal bankruptcy case in history.

The county had hoped bankruptcy protection would buy time to work out a financial restructuring that would avoid a bond default, or a lender's inability to meet a bond's regularly scheduled interest or principal payments.

Municipal bonds, popular investments...

> **Victims of Orange County's financial crisis include kids who won court settlements, whose parents were advised by judges to invest in the county fund. Page 2F**

DESIGNER
CHAD HAGEN
MINNEAPOLIS
MINNESOTA

TYPOGRAPHIC SOURCE
IN-HOUSE

STUDIO
THORBURN
DESIGN

CLIENT
CONCERTS
FOR THE
ENVIRONMENT

PRINCIPAL TYPES
TRADE GOTHIC
AND CUSTOM

DIMENSIONS
13 x 20 IN.
(33 x 50.8 CM)
POSTER

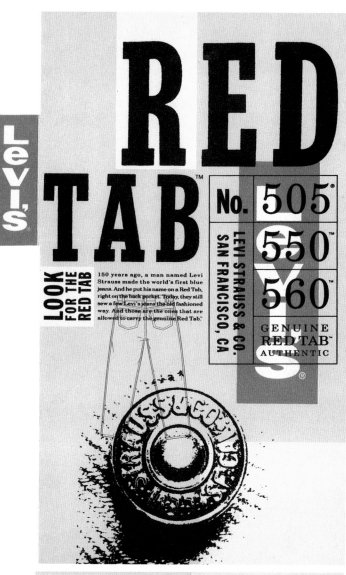

LOOK FOR THE RED TAB™

150 years ago, a man named Levi Strauss made the world's first blue jeans. And he put his name on a Red Tab, right on the back pocket. Today, they still sew a few Levi's jeans the old fashioned way. And those are the ones that are allowed to carry the genuine Red Tab.™

DESIGNER
STEVEN
SANDSTROM
PORTLAND OREGON

TYPOGRAPHIC SOURCES
IN-HOUSE AND
A BUNCH OF
CHARACTERS

AGENCY
FOOTE CONE &
BELDING/SAN
FRANCISCO

STUDIO
SANDSTROM
DESIGN, INC.

CLIENT
LEVI STRAUSS & CO.

PRINCIPAL TYPES
CENTURY
SCHOOLBOOK,
FRANKLIN
GOTHIC, AND
STYMIE

DIMENSIONS
4 x 7 IN.
(10.2 x 17.8 CM)

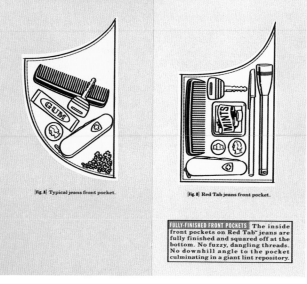

[Fig. 8] Typical jeans front pocket.

[Fig. 8] Red Tab jeans front pocket.

FULLY-FINISHED FRONT POCKETS The inside front pockets on Red Tab™ jeans are fully finished and squared off at the bottom. No fuzzy, dangling threads. No downhill angle to the pocket culminating in a giant lint repository.

DESIGNERS
BROCK
HALDEMAN AND
JIM LARMON
CHICAGO ILLINOIS

TYPOGRAPHIC SOURCE
IN-HOUSE

STUDIO
PIVOT DESIGN,
INC.

CLIENT
THE
PHOTOGRAPHIC
STUDIO OF
STEVEN
McDONALD

PRINCIPAL TYPES
BODONI OPEN,
BOOKMAN, AND
COPPERPLATE
GOTHIC

DIMENSIONS
8½ x 11 IN.
(21.6 x 27.9 CM)

DESIGNERSS
MICHAEL BIERUT,
SEYMOUR
CHWAST, FUKUDA
SHIGEO, PAULA
SCHER, AND
PIERRE MENDELL
NEW YORK NEW YORK
AND VARIOUS OTHERS

CALLIGRAPHER
VARIOUS

LETTERER
VARIOUS

ART DIRECTOR
PAULA SCHER

TYPOGRAPHIC SOURCE
IN-HOUSE

STUDIO
PENTAGRAM
DESIGN

CLIENTS
AMBASSADOR
ARTS AND
CHAMPION
INTERNATIONAL
CORPORATION

PRINCIPAL TYPE
VARIOUS

DIMENSIONS
23 x 35 IN.
(58 x 88.9 CM)

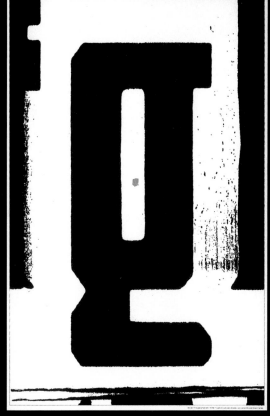

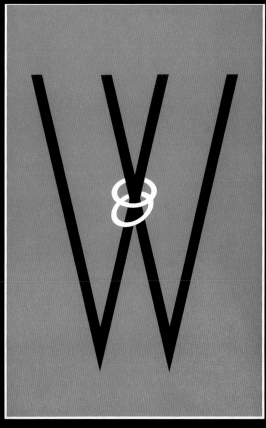

AptarGroup
annual
1993
report

finger-actuated **dispensing**
Pumps
systems **for products ranging from** fine-mist
sprays to lotions

...es of pumps and
...place challenges
...s on continuous
...both Europe and
...lization provides
...arket. Indeed, we
...market. We are
...cosmetics market.
...m personal care,
...sistent across all
...ding quality and
...ource is our stable
...d will continue to
...d entrepreneurial
...ities of the future.

...ting Officer

DESIGNERS
GREG SAMATA
AND
DAN KRAEMER
DUNDEE ILLINOIS

TYPOGRAPHIC SOURCE
IN-HOUSE

AGENCY
SAMATA
ASSOCIATES

CLIENT
APTARGROUP

PRINCIPAL TYPES
UNIVERS AND
BODONI

DIMENSIONS
$7^{5}/_{8}$ X $11^{3}/_{4}$ IN.
(19.4 X 29.8 CM)

iT's
Not Just
ROCK AND
ROLL

" Musicland isn't *just* rock 'n' roll anymore. Actually, it never was. Growing up in the glory years of Ella Fitzgerald, Elvis Presley, and the Beatles, Musicland Stores Corporation made its reputation by offering audiophiles the widest selection of prerecorded music available anywhere. Nearly 40 years later, many of the big names have changed - Nirvana, Whitney Houston, Garth MUSICLAND STORES CORPORATION Brooks - but we're still a leader in the sale of prerecorded music products. We've also become a fast-growing force in "full-media" retailing. Today's Musicland Stores Corporation is music *plus* video *plus* books *plus* computer software.

In 1993 we continued to build the company on the solid foundation of our mall-based music and video businesses. We achieved significant growth with the addition of 12 full-media Media Play superstores in non-mall locations in major and mid-size metropolitan areas and with 19 smaller full-media On Cue stores in smaller markets. We increased our overall retail square footage by 1.1 million, expanded into new geographic areas, and broadened our product line.

The Company solidified its financial position with a successful public stock offering that increased equity by $70.7 million and by retiring our high-cost debt through an offering of new debt at lower interest rates. We not only had a solid year in 1993, but also entered 1994 ready to make the most of the hottest retailing trends in the home-entertainment industry. **1993 ANNUAL REPORT**

For the year ended December 31, 1993, Company sales rose to $1.18 billion, an increase of 15.8 percent over itan areas and with 19 smaller full-media On Cue stores in smaller markets.

The full-media shopping environment generated by **Media Play** in large and medium markets also is available on a smaller scale in smaller markets, such as Spencer, Iowa, and Norfolk, Nebraska. Here the store is called On Cue. With 20,000 compact discs, cassettes, books, videos, accessories, and apparel displayed for interactive browsing and shopping in about 6,200 square feet of retail space, it's only the size of the store, not the experience, that's been reduced.

On Cue stores are designed for markets of between 10,000 and 50,000 people and of more than an hour drive from the nearest regional shopping center. Typically situated near the community's main shopping hub, On Cue stores combine the friendly coziness of a specialty shop with a breadth of product, service, and amenities unavailable elsewhere in the area. A store's inventory will usually include 6,500 compact discs and cassettes, 10,000 book titles, 3,500 movies, hundreds of magazines and comic books, and a wide selection of entertainment-licensed products such as t-shirts, caps, key chains, and toys.

All On Cue stores are committed to the principle "Big Selection, Small Price." And the excitement doesn't end with the merchandise. Take the small-town general store of days past, On Cue stores operate as center of updated, family-oriented community activity. Autograph parties featuring popular authors and artists, appearances by costumed children's characters, and previews of new music, video, and book releases are typical On Cue events.

The first On Cue store was opened in Fairmont, Minnesota, in early 1992, and by year-end 1993 the total store count was 57. Because of the enthusiastic response to On Cue during 1993, Musicland Stores Corporation plans to open more than 30 new stores by the end of 1994.

Why should big cities have all the fun?

ON CUE

P. 10

VIRGINIA AND GEORGE SICKLER George Sickler has lived on the same 360-acre farm near Dunnell, Minnesota (pop. 187) all his life. Together with Virginia, his wife, he raises corn, soybeans, and hogs in the richest occupations on earth. Because Virginia "needs anything she gets her hands on," George says, and because he is an avid movie collector, they split their media-shopping time between On Cue stores in Fairmont, Minnesota, and Spencer, Iowa. George scrambles out westerns and action movies released from 1945 to 1955; he recently bought *Action in the North Atlantic* with Humphrey Bogart. They buy, George says, "because it's a drive into town to rent, and to go to a movie costs us $4 a person and you gotta buy popcorn." And, he adds, "there are no westerns now. We go to On Cue because the prices are lower and the selection is poor in other places. A clerk at one of the other stores told us about On Cue, and we've been going there ever since. I just saw Rich On Cue store managers) at Spencer last week."

Otto, and St. Cloud, Minnesota. By the end of this year, the Company expects to have 45 or more Media Play stores in full operation.

A typical Media Play store offers customers an unequaled mix of 40,000 music titles, 40,000 book titles, 12,000 movie and specialty video titles, 1,000 computer-software programs, 17 magazine titles, 200 comic books, and hundreds of accessory items, greeting cards, and licensed music, movie, and sports apparel.

But Media Play is not a musty warehouse stocked high with a confusion of merchandise. Media Play is a bright, attractive, browsing-friendly shopping environment expressly designed to match the interests, tastes, and lifestyles of Baby Boomers and their families.

Each Media Play store offers dozens of interactive preview stations where customers may listen, view, and peruse at their leisure. Customers may look and sample to their heart's content, and if they want help, knowledgeable employees are there to give it. A special children's section provides entertainment and education for kids. Stores represent programs devoted to important community concerns like fitness and safety, as well as frequent author signings, performances, and kids' story hours. under that in many locations Media became a neighborhood gathering are many visitors spend more than in the first time they stop by. Media a media playground for all ages.

MEDIA PLAY

P. 7

What do you call a 50,000-square-foot superstore where you can shop for the latest in prerecorded music and movies, books and magazines, computer software, even lovely apparel with entertainment themes - all at low prices and with the help of personal, professional service? Call it Media Play, a full-media shopping experience.

With the opening of its first Media Play superstore in Rockford, Illinois, in late 1992, Musicland Stores Corporation introduced the full-media shopping concept to America. The concept spotlights the wide-ranging, often overlapping media interests the Baby Boom generation demands of a home-entertainment store and showcases these interests in a huge, one-stop inviting location.

THE KAPALAS Jill and Fred Kapala and their daughters Katie, 9, and Candy, 6, live a busy life in Rockford, Illinois. Trying to find spare time amid hectic school and work schedules—Fred is an associate judge and Jill is a homemaker and substitute teacher—presents an all too common challenge for the family.

All the family members enjoy reading, and so a ritual has evolved since a Media Play opened near their home in late 1992. "We often go on Friday nights - our night out - to Media Play," Jill says. "We go to buy books and then come home and have reading time together. When I go into Media Play and see all the books available for kids, I wonder why we have a television."

These days, Katie is into The Baby-Sitters Club series and gravitates towards Mariah Carey's music. Fred often grabs a magazine, and the other two Kapalas search for a variety of titles.

"We see lots of people we know at Media Play," Jill adds. "It's really a family place."

top **10**

DESIGNERS
AMY QUINLIVAN
AND SHARON
WERNER
MINNEAPOLIS
MINNESOTA

LETTERERS
AMY QUINLIVAN
AND SHARON
WERNER

TYPOGRAPHIC SOURCE
IN-HOUSE

AGENCY
MUSICLAND
STORES
CORPORATION

STUDIO
QUINLIVAN/
WERNER
DESIGN WERKS

CLIENT
MUSICLAND
STORES
CORPORATION

PRINCIPAL TYPES
TRADE AND
CLARENDON
BOOK

DIMENSIONS
8½ X 11 IN.
(21.6 X 27.9 CM)

DESIGNERS
DAVID J. HWANG
AND BILL
DAWSON
HOLLYWOOD
CALIFORNIA

TYPOGRAPHIC SOURCE
IN-HOUSE

STUDIO
TWO HEADED
MONSTER

CLIENT
KCET

PRINCIPAL TYPES
TRAJAN AND
FRANKLIN
GOTHIC HEAVY

DESIGNERS
NEIL POWELL
AND ALAN
LEUSINK
MINNEAPOLIS
MINNESOTA

LETTERER
NEIL POWELL

TYPOGRAPHIC SOURCE
IN-HOUSE

STUDIO
DUFFY DESIGN

CLIENT
THE STROH
BREWERY
COMPANY

PRINCIPAL TYPES
20TH CENTURY
GOTHIC AND
IONIC BOLD

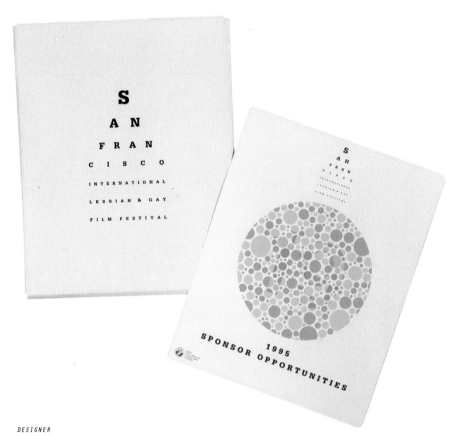

DESIGNER
DAVID
SALANITRO
SAN FRANCISCO
CALIFORNIA

TYPOGRAPHIC SOURCE
IN-HOUSE

STUDIO
OH BOY, A
DESIGN
COMPANY

CLIENT
FRAMELINE

PRINCIPAL TYPES
GLYPHA,
ATSACKERS,
AND GOTHIC
MEDIUM

DIMENSIONS
8 X 10 IN.
(20.3 X 25.4 CM)

DESIGNER
UWE LOESCH
DÜSSELDORF GERMANY

TYPOGRAPHIC SOURCE
IN-HOUSE

CLIENT
IBA EMSCHER
PARK

PRINCIPAL TYPE
UNIVERS BOLD

DIMENSIONS
33¹/₁₆ X 47⁷/₈ IN.
(84 X 119 CM)

Das Industriezeitalter im Ruhrgebiet

Von oben und von unten ___

Eine Ausstellung im Gasometer Oberhausen

15. Juli bis 1. November 1994

Feuer

Flamma

&

DESIGNER
SAKOL
MONGKOLKASETARIN
NEWPORT BEACH CALIFORNIA

LETTERER
SAKOL
MONGKOLKASETARIN

TYPOGRAPHIC SOURCE
IN-HOUSE

AGENCY
ACME ADVERTISING

CLIENT
ACME ADVERTISING

COPYWRITER
BRIAN WEST

PRINCIPAL TYPE
NEW CALEDONIA

DIMENSIONS
8¹/₂ x 11 in.
(21.6 x 27.9 cm)

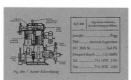

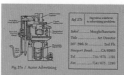

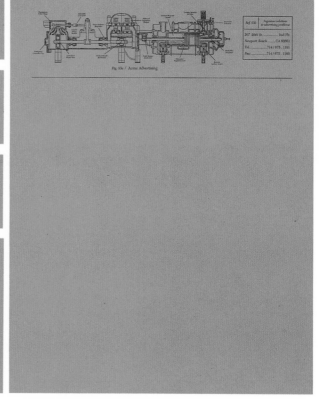

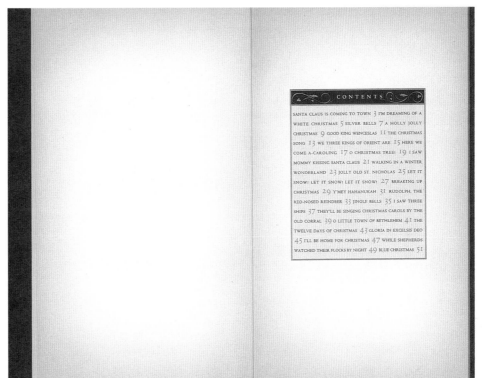

DESIGNERS
JANET KRUSE,
TRACI DABERKO,
AND DENNIS
CLOUSE
SEATTLE WASHINGTON

TYPOGRAPHIC SOURCE
IN-HOUSE

STUDIO
THE LEONHARDT
GROUP

CLIENT
PAT HACKETT

PRINCIPAL TYPE
MONOTYPE
CENTAUR

DIMENSIONS
4³/₄ x 7¹/₂ IN.
(12.1 x 19.1 CM)

VIKKI LEIB

Computer

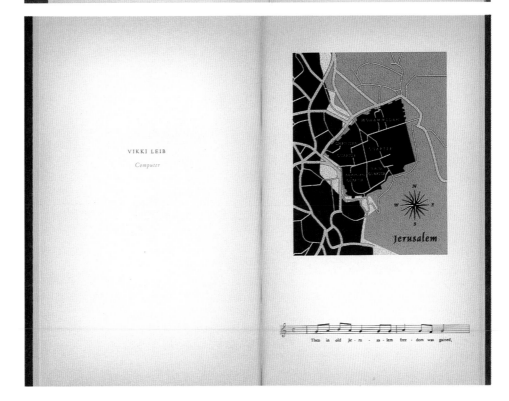

DESIGNERS
**ROBERT WONG
AND ARTURO
AVANDA**
NEW YORK NEW YORK

TYPOGRAPHIC SOURCE
IN-HOUSE

AGENCY
**FRANKFURT
BALKIND
PARTNERS**

CLIENT
**THE LIMITED,
INC.**

PRINCIPAL TYPE
HELVETICA

DESIGNER
UWE LOESCH
DÜSSELDORF GERMANY

TYPOGRAPHIC SOURCE
IN-HOUSE

CLIENT
**THE ISRAEL
MUSEUM
JERUSALEM**

PRINCIPAL TYPE
FRUTIGER BOLD

DIMENSIONS
46⅞ x 66⅛ IN.
(119 x 168 CM)

POSTER

The Place, the Time and the Point, Posters by Uwe Loesch

The Israel Museum, Jerusalem, Palevsky Design Pavilion   22 February – 30 April 199

TYPE DIRECTORS CLUB

258 TYPE DIRECTORS CLUB

BOARD OF DIRECTORS 1994/95

Officers

President — *B. Martin Pedersen, Graphis*

Vice President — *Mara Kurtz, Mara Kurtz Studio*

Secretary/Treasurer — *Mark Solsburg, FontHaus Inc.*

Directors-at-Large — *Kathie Brown, U.S. Lithograph, typographers*

Ed Colker, The Cooper Union

Cynthia Hollandsworth, Agfa Division, Bayer Corp.

Gerard Huerta, Gerard Huerta Design, Inc.

Daniel Pelavin, Daniel Pelavin

Dirk Rowntree, Young & Rubicam New York

Ilene Strizver, International Typeface Corporation

Chairperson, Board of Directors — *Allan Haley, Resolution*

BOARD OF DIRECTORS 1995/96

Officers

President — *B. Martin Pedersen, Graphis*

Vice President — *Mara Kurtz, Mara Kurtz Studio*

Secretary/Treasurer — *Mark Solsburg, FontHaus Inc.*

Directors-at-Large — *Adam Greiss, Adam Greiss Design*

Kathie Brown, U.S. Lithograph, typographers

Cynthia Hollandsworth, Agfa Division, Bayer Corp.

Gerard Huerta, Gerard Huerta Design, Inc.

Daniel Pelavin, Daniel Pelavin

Paul Shaw, Paul Shaw Design

Richard Wilde, School of Visual Arts

Chairperson, Board of Directors — *Allan Haley, Resolution*

COMMITTEE FOR TDC 41

Chairperson — *Mara Kurtz*

Design — *Drenttel Doyle Partners*

Coordinator — *Carol Wahler*

Assistant Coordinator — *Klaus Schmidt*

Calligrapher — *Robert Boyajian*

Assistants to Judges — *Peter Bain, Laurie Burns, Cristina Canlas, Carol DeBlasio, Adam Greiss, Bonnie Hazelton, Judith Kazdym Leeds, Michael Milley, Eric Neuner, Nancy Romano, Nicole Salzone, Geraldine Schoeller, Agatha Sohn, Ed Vadala, Adam Wahler, Allan R. Wahler, Samantha Wahler, and Aziz Zizoune.*

TDC PRESIDENTS

Frank Powers, 1946, 1947

Milton Zudeck, 1948

Alfred Dickman, 1949

Joseph Weiler, 1950

James Secrest, 1951, 1952, 1953

Gustave Saelens, 1954, 1955

Arthur Lee, 1956, 1957

Martin Connell, 1958

James Secrest, 1959, 1960

Frank Powers, 1961, 1962

Milton Zudeck, 1963, 1964

Gene Ettenberg, 1965, 1966

Edward Gottschall, 1967, 1968

Saadyah Maximon, 1969

Louis Lepis, 1970, 1971

Gerard O'Neill, 1972, 1973

Zoltan Kiss, 1974, 1975

Roy Zucca, 1976, 1977

William Streever, 1978, 1979

Bonnie Hazelton, 1980, 1981

Jack George Tauss, 1982, 1983

Klaus F. Schmidt, 1984, 1985

John Luke, 1986, 1987

Jack Odette, 1988, 1989

Ed Benguiat, 1990, 1991

Allan Haley, 1992, 1993

B. Martin Pedersen, 1994, 1995

TDC MEDAL RECIPIENTS

Hermann Zapf, 1967

R. Hunter Middleton, 1968

Frank Powers, 1971

Dr. Robert Leslie, 1972

Edward Rondthaler, 1975

Arnold Bank, 1979

Georg Trump, 1982

Paul Standard, 1983

Herb Lubalin, 1984 (posthumously)

Paul Rand, 1984

Aaron Burns, 1985

Bradbury Thompson, 1986

Adrian Frutiger, 1987

Freeman Craw, 1988

Ed Benguiat, 1989

Gene Federico, 1991

SPECIAL CITATIONS TO TDC MEMBERS

Edward Gottschall, 1955

Freeman Craw, 1968

James Secrest, 1974

Olaf Leu, 1984, 1990

William Streever, 1984

Klaus F. Schmidt, 1985

John Luke, 1987

Jack Odette, 1989

1995 SCHOLARSHIP RECIPIENTS

Jason Andrew Brightman, Pratt Institute

Kaming Liu, The Cooper Union

David Byun, School of Visual Arts

Irene Santoso, Parsons School of Design

Carol Wahler, Executive Director

Type Directors Club
60 East 42nd Street, Suite 721
New York, NY 10165

212-983-6042
FAX 212-983-6043

For membership information please
contact the Type Directors Club offices.

INTERNATIONAL LIAISON CHAIRPERSONS

ENGLAND
David Farey
HouseStyle
50-54 Clerkenwell Road
London EC1M 5PS

FRANCE
Christopher Dubber
Signum Art
94, Avenue Victor Hugo
94100 Saint Maur Des Fosses

GERMANY
Bertram Schmidt-Friderichs
Universitatsdruckerei und Verlag
H. Schmidt GmbH & Co.
Robert Koch Strasse 8
Postfach 42 07 28
55129 Mainz Hechtsheim

JAPAN
Japan Typography Association
C C Center
4-8-15 Yushima
Bunkyo-ku
Tokyo 113

MEXICO
Prof. Felix Beltran
Apartado de Correos
M 10733 Mexico 06000

REPUBLIC OF SINGAPORE
Gordon Tan
Gordon Tan Academy
#3 Jaian Pisang
Singapore 0719

SOUTH AMERICA
Diego Vainesman
160 East 26 Street
New York, New York 10010

SWEDEN
Ernst Dernehl
Dernehl & Son Designers
Box 8073
S-10420 Stockholm

Jim Aitchison '93

Victor Ang '91

Martyn Anstice '92

Hal Apple '94

Herman Aronson '92

Robyn Gill Attaway '93

Peter Bain '86

Bruce Balkin '93

Maria Helena Ferreira
   Braga Barbosa '93s

Clarence Baylis '74

Felix Beltran '88

Ed Benguiat '64

Randall Bennett '94

Jesse Berger '92

Anna Berkenbusch '89

Peter Bertolami '69

Klaus Bietz '93

Roger Black '80

Anthony Bloch '88

Susan Cotler Block '89

Karlheinz Boelling '86

Garrett Boge '83

Patricia Bradbury '93

Bud Braman '90

Risa Brand '94

Ed Brodsky '80

Kathie Brown '84

Bill Bundzak '64

Queenie Burns '94

Elizabeth Butler '94s

Jason Calfo '88

Ronn Campisi '88

Cristina Canlas '93

Matthew Carter '88

Ken Cato '88

Petra Cerne '94s

Theseus Chan '94

Herman Chandra '94s

Len Cheeseman '93

Kai-Yan Choi '90

Tae Gil Chung '94s

Traci Churchill '95

Andrew Clarke '93

Travis Cliett '53

Mahlon A. Cline* '48

Tom Cocozza '76

Lisa Cohen '93

Angelo Colella '90

Ed Colker '83

Paul Correia '93

Freeman Craw* '47

Jennifer Crupi '94s

David Cundy '85

Leonard Currie '93

Rick Cusick '89

Luiz Dalomba '94

Susan Darbyshire '87

Ismar David '58

Lisa David '95s

Don Davidson '93

Ashley Davis '95s

Richard Dawson '93

Carol DeBlasio 94s

Matej Decko '93

Robert Defrin '69

Heather Dega '94s

Josanne De Natale '86

Ernst Dernehl '87

Claude Dieterich '84

Lou Dorfsman '54

Anthony Douglas '94

Kyle Dreier '94

John Dreyfus** '68

Christopher Dubber '85

Lutz Dziarnowski '92

Rick Eiber '85

Friedrich Eisenmenger '93

Dr. Elsi Vassdal Ellis '93

Garry Emery '93

Nick Ericson '92

Joseph Michael Essex '78

Leslie Evans '92

Florence Everett '89

Peter Fahrni '93

David Farey '93

Michael Farmer '94

Gene Federico** '91

Simon Fitton '94

Kristine Fitzgerald '90

Mona Fitzgerald '91

Yvonne Fitzner '87

Norbert Florendo '84

Vincent Fong '93s

Gonçalo Fonseca '93

Alex Fornari '94

Tony Forster '88

Thomas Fowler '93

Dean Franklin '80

Carol Freed '87

Adrian Frutiger ** '67

Partick Fultz '87

Gene Gable '95

Murray Gaby '93

Fred Gardner '92

Christof Gassner '90

David Gatti '81

Jeremy Gee '92

Ginger Geist '95

Stuart Germain '74

Lou Glassheim * '47

Howard Glener '77

Laurie Goldman '93s

Harriet Goren '94

Edward Gottschall '52

Norman Graber '69

Diana Graham '85

Austin Grandjean '59

Kevin Greenblat '93s

Adam Greiss '89

Jeff Griffith '91

Rosanne Guararra '92

Dante B. Guintu '94s

Kurt Haiman '82

Allan Haley '78

Sherri Harnick '83

John Harrison '91

Knut Hartmann '85

Nabeel Kamal

    Hassan '94

Bonnie Hazelton '75

Jeri Heiden '94

Richard Henderson '92

Klaus Hesse '95

Jay Higgins '88

Elise Hilpert '89

Michael Hodgson '89

Fritz Hofrichter '80

Alyce Hoggan '91

Cynthia

    Hollandsworth '91

Catherine

    Hollenbeck '93

Kevin Horvath '87

Gerard Huerta '85

Harvey Hunt '92

Anthony A. Inciong '93s

Elizabeth Irwin '94s

Donald Jackson ** '78

Michael Jager '94

John Jamilkowski '89

Jon Jicha '87

Iskra Johnson '94

Anita Karl '94

Karen Kassirer '93

Scott Kelly '84

Michael O. Kelly '84

Renée Khatami '90

Hermann Kilian '92

Rick King '93

Zoltan Kiss '59

Robert C. Knecht '69

Nana Kobayashi '94s

Seiko Kohjima '95s

Myosook Koo '93s

Steve Kopec '74

Michelle Koza '94

Andrej Krátky '93

Bernhard J. Kress '63

Madhu Krishna '91

Pat Krugman '91

Ralf Kunz '93

Mara Kurtz '89

Sasha Kurtz '91s

Misook Kwak '93s

Gerry L'Orange '91

Raymond F. Laccetti '87

Julia Katja Lachnik '94s

John Langdon '93

Guenter Gerhard

Lange '83

Judith Kazdym Leeds '83

Olaf Leu '65

Jeffery Level '88

Mark Lichtenstein '84

Ginny Lindzey '94a

Wally Littman '60

John Howland

    Lord ** '47

Alexander Luckow '94

Gregg Lukasiewicz '90

John Luke '78

Burns Magruder '93

Sol Malkoff '63

Daniela Mandil '95

Marilyn Marcus '79

David Marino '94s

Adolfo Martinez '86

Rogério Martins '91

Deborah Masel '94s

Les Mason '85

Douglas May '92

Roland Mehler '92

Frédéric Metz '85

Douglas Michalek '77

Michael Milley '94s

John Milligan '78

Michael Miranda '84

Oswaldo Miranda

    (Miran) '78

Sotiris Mitroussis '94

Nancy Molins '94s

James Montalbano '93

Richard Moore '82

Denis Moriarty '94

Minoru Morita '75

Gerald Moscato '93

Tobias Moss * '47

James Mowrey '95

Richard Mullen '82

Antonio Muñoz '90

Keith Murgatroyd '78

Jerry King Musser '88

Alexander Musson '93

Louis A. Musto '65

Alexander Nesbitt '50

Julie Nishosian '94

Robert Norton '92

Alexa Nosal '87

Robert O'Connor '92

Brian O'Neill '68

Jack Odette '77

Michel Olivier '94

Robert Overholtzer '94

Bob Paganucci '85

Susan Panetta '95

Jim Parkinson '94

B. Martin Pedersen '85

Daniel Pelavin '92

Robert Peters '86

Peter Hans

    Pfaffmann '94

Roy Podorson '77

William Porch '94

Will Powers '89

Vittorio Prina '88

Richard Puder '85

David Quay '80

Elissa Querzé '83

Erwin Raith '67

Diddo Ramm '95

Adeir Rampazzo '85

Paul Rand ** '86
Hermann Rapp '87
Jo Anne Redwood '88
Hans Dieter
    Reichert '92
Bud Renshaw '83
Martha Rhodes '93
Robert Ripp '93ʌ
Nancy Romano '93ʌ
Salvadore Romero '94
Edward Rondthaler* '47
Kurt Roscoe '93
Robert M. Rose '75
Daryl Roske '94
Dirk Rowntree '86
Joanne Rudden-
    Barsky '94
Erkki Ruuhinen '86
Michael Rylander '93
Gus Saelens '50
Howard J. Salberg '87
David Saltman '66
Richard Sasso '94
Frank Sax '94
Hermann
    J. Schlieper '87
Hermann Schmidt '83
Klaus Schmidt '59
Markus Schmidt '93
Michael Schmidt '95
Peter Schmidt '93ʌ
Bertram Schmidt-
    Friderichs '89
Werner Schneider '87
Eileen Hedy Schultz '85
Eckehart Schumacher-

Gebler '85
Paul Shaw '87
Philip Shore, Jr. '92
Robin Siegel '94
Gil A. Silva '92
Mark Simkins '92
Scott Simmons '94
Arlyn Simon '95
Mondrey Sin '95
Tyler Singer '93
Dwight D. A. Smith '92
Kimberly Smith '93ʌ
Felix Sockwell '95
Martin Solomon '55
Jan Solpera '85
Mark Solsburg '89
Barbara Sommer '92
Ronnie Tan Soo Chye '88
Bill Sosin '92
Erik Spiekermann '88
Vic Spindler '73
Walter Stanton '58
Rolf Staudt '84
Thomas Stecko '94
Charles Stewart '92
Sumner Stone '88
William Streever '50
Ilene Strizver '88
Hansjorg Stulle '87
Tony Sutton '93
Zempaku Suzuki '92
Gunnar Swanson '92
Ken Sweeny '78
Paul Sych '93
Gordon Tan '90
Michael Tardif '92

William Taubin '56
Jack Tauss '75
Pat Taylor '85
Anthony J. Teano '62
Mark Tenga '93
Grover Tham '93
Bradbury Thompson '58
Paula Thomson '91
Eric Tilley '95
Joseph Treacy '94
Harry Title '93
D. A. Tregidga '85
Pat Troso '94ʌ
Susan B. Trowbridge '82
Lucile Tuttle-Smith '78
Edward Vadala '72
Diego Vainesman '91
Violeta Valle '94ʌ
Mark van Bronkhorst '93
Jan Van Der Ploeg '52
Pamela Vassil '95
James Wageman '88
Frank Wagner '94
Jurek Wajdowicz '80
Robert Wakeman '85
Garth Walker '92
Tat S. Wan '91
Xu Wang '93
Ewan Warmbath '93
Janet Webb '91
Joy Weeeng '93ʌ
Kurt Weidemann '66
Seth Weine '95
Alex White '93
Gail Wiggin '90
Richard Wilde '93

James Williams '88
Carol Winer '94
Conny J. Winter '85
Michelle Winters '93ʌ
Shen-Hua Yen '95ʌ
Teresa Yeung '94ʌ
Doyald Young '94
Shawn Young '94
Susan Young '93
Hermann Zapf ** '52
Roy Zucca '69

SUSTAINING MEMBERS

Adobe Systems, Inc. '90
Badillo Nazca
    Saatchi & Saatchi '94
International Typeface
    Corporation '80
Letraset '91
Linotype-Hell Company '63
Monotype Typography,
    Inc. '91

*   Charter member
** Honorary member
ʌ   Student member
a   Associate member

Membership as
    of May 31, 1995

INDEX

THE FORTY–FIRST ANNUAL **TYPE DIRECTORS CLUB** EXHIBITION

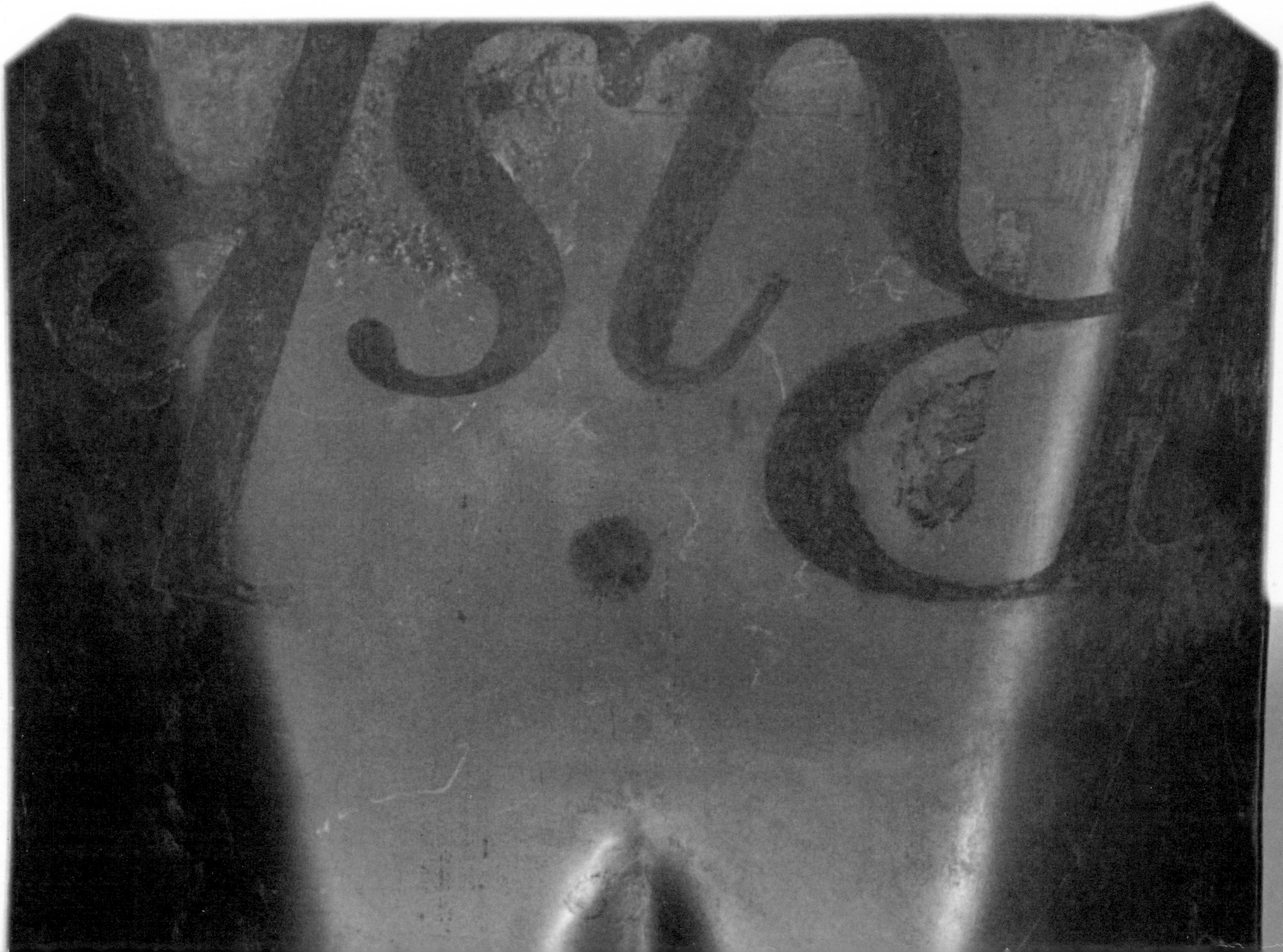